MALE *Sexual* ENDURANCE

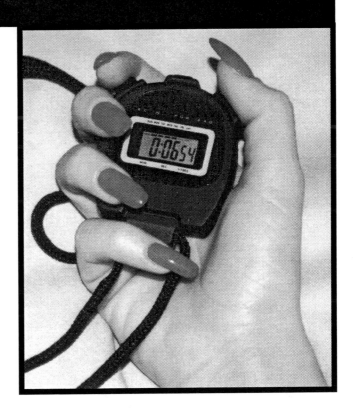

Robert W. Birch, Ph.D., FAACS

Psychologist

Marital & Sex Therapist

MALE SEXUAL ENDURANCE: A Man's Book About Ejaculatory Control

ISBN: 1-57074-349-5

Other Publications by the author:

Oral Caress: The Loving Guide to Exciting A Woman
ISBN: 1-57074-307-X   [1996]

A Sex Therapist's Manual
ISBN: 1-57074-320-7   [1996]

Printed in the United States of America

PEC Publishing
28 W. Henderson Road
Columbus, OH 43214-2628

Library of Congress Cataloging-in-Publication Data:
Birch, Robert W.
Male Sexual Endurance
1. Premature Ejaculation 2. Sex Therapy 3. Male Sexuality 4. Sex Instruction for Men 5. Sexual Dysfunction

The sexual acts portrayed are simulations by consenting adults 21 years of age or older. Records are maintained by the author.

Dedicated to all our sons...

and to their sons.

Acknowledgments

Appreciation is expressed to Cynthia Lief Ruberg, M.S.Ed., AASECT Certified Sex Counselor, for her helpful content and editorial comments, and to Cindy Kingery for her kind patience and skilled technical assistance. My wife Susan has been a constant source of encouragement and her unwavering support should not go unnoted.

TABLE OF CONTENTS

INTRODUCTION
MALE SEXUAL ENDURANCE:

A MAN'S BOOK ABOUT EJACULATORY CONTROL

At first glance, this book might appear to be more about the evolution of male mating behavior than it is about human love. Admittedly I begin my exploration of rapid ejaculation by first wondering what ejaculation was all about in prehistoric days. Modern man, as we know him today, is quite different from those distant ancestors who sought their shelter in caves. However, we do have many things in common with these distant relatives... including the male penis and the desire to use it. It is only within fairly recent time that man has used his penis to make love as well as to make babies. Not so with our ancient ancestors. Is there something, therefore, to be learned about the origin of rapid ejaculation by considering our forefathers' use of sex?

My book is written from the perspective of a sexologist with 30 years of experience in working with the emotional and sexual concerns of modern day people... sensitive people who value love and companionship, who search for intimacy as readily as they search for pleasure. Ultimately as you read my book you will discover that this manuscript is about sharing joy, but you will first need to bear with me as we wonder through the biological and mechanical background.

Some who read my book might get the idea that I am downplaying the importance of intercourse and condoning those unintentional "quickies." Nothing could be further from the truth. However, I do not view intercourse as being the only expression of intimate behavior... nor necessarily the most pleasurable behavior for some men and women. I do not agree that *making intercourse* is the same as *making love* and I hope you will come to understand my emphasis on the *process* of giving and receiving pleasure as opposed to a focus on the *goal* of having an orgasm. Am I saying that coming should not be important? No, not at all, but what I am saying is that ultimately the focus of making love should be on the joyful sharing of erotic pleasure... intercourse and orgasms hopefully included but not required.

This is not a book about a "cure" for premature ejaculation, as I do not view this as an illness, nor necessarily as a problem. Although it may certainly be an inconvenience, it is not a catastrophe! It is unfortunate that one author referred to "the victims of premature ejaculation." I want to undo this idea of a horrible infliction and talk instead of a very positive orgasm that just happens to occur early in an encounter.

I will make no claims that in X number of weeks you will be capable of merrily thrusting away without the fear of ever again coming too soon. What I will tell you is that I believe there is something very natural about reaching orgasm quickly, but that there are ways to work with this to achieve better management of that ejaculatory reflex. I will warn you that if you are a true premature ejaculator, you will need to be mindful of what I tell you... for most of the rest of your life.

I wish I could have written that book entitled *"How to Cure Premature Ejaculation in Seven Short Days."* I'd make a million! However, the research on the effectiveness of the traditional treatment of premature ejaculation is somewhat disappointing. Despite what I consider to be exaggerated claims by overjealous professionals, various follow up studies seem to yield discouraging results with regard to success. It is just not clear how well the old approaches have worked or how long any improvements would last. It has been found that most men, contacted a few years after their treatment had ended, seemed to have lost whatever gains that had been made! Fear not! I believe that the loss of progress is high because most approaches promise a cure and once it seems to have taken place, everyone gets careless, old patterns of behavior return, and the problem comes back! I'm not surprised!

I have had men become angry with me because I have been unable to give them a quick fix. Unfortunately, there is nothing easy or quick. Thus, I ask for your patience in learning how to manage your sexual excitement. There is a wise old

Chinese proverb that says, "*Give a man a fish and he'll eat today. Teach a man to fish and he'll eat forever!*" It is my intent to look at rapid ejaculation from many different perspectives, to review what has been tried in the past, to instruct you in things to do, and I hope to teach you how to forever monitor and control your ejaculatory function. Sorry guys, I make no promises about this weekend... while you may find some helpful tidbit for handling that hot date, it is my intent to go for the more reliable long term rewards!

Chapter 1

BEGINNING TO UNDERSTAND

THE BASICS: EJACULATION 101

For eons, primate males have roamed restlessly over our earth, driven by two basic and primitive instincts These powerful primary drives are themselves quite simple; the instinct to *survive* and instinct to *procreate* (by necessity, in that precise order). In the wild, the fulfillment of these needs is not always easy, the behaviors involved are not always direct, and the outcome is not always predictable. The purpose of the behavior may not be apparent and the action taken to accomplish the goal can be quite intricate. This is particularly true when we begin talking of the complicated behavior of the anything-but-primitive <u>human</u> male who now lives in a highly complex social environment.

In contemporary human society, man's basic survival has become relatively easy. With the absence of man-eating predators, with ample food to fill his belly, and with adequate shelter when the environment turns hostile, modern-day man turns his energies to many less essential forms of security (status, money, etc.). There is a sense of protection and safety within which the second basic drive (procreation) can readily find expression... and modern man adds much more emotion and psychological meaning to this primitive "urge to merge."

It is interesting and significant that human beings are the only members of the animal kingdom who engage in intercourse for reasons other than procreation and who do so regardless of where the female is in her cycle of egg production. All other animals copulate only when the female is in estrus, when eggs are present and the chance of impregnation is greatest. In lower animals, the drive to procreate is strong, mating occurs when the time is right and life miraculously reproduces itself. With human couples, the drive is also strong, but copulation occurs at any time, and great effort is usually taken to actually avoid conception. Human beings engage in intercourse for both *procreation* and *recreation*... but with much more emphasis focus on the latter!

This strong drive to mate, the powerful urge to merge, is innate. It is built in. It is hard-wired into our electro-chemical system. We did not learn the instinct, although our environment, our society and our chemistry have collectively shaped the behavior we employ to satisfy this drive. In nature, the male instinct is to deposit millions of sperm in one dose within the female, so that these agile swimmers might follow their predetermined course to fertilize any eggs present. With human males this desire to ejaculate is somewhat independent of opportunities and relationships, and therefore, in the absence of a partner, masturbation is often used to satisfy this biological hunger. As some theologies would remind us, in this solitary act, semen is spilled without the remotest chance of a pregnancy. Now is not the time nor place, however, to argue whether this is sinful or expedient, immoral or simply convenient. The author's intent is only to remind the reader that the drive to ejaculate is inborn and this need for sexual release can become quite demanding. Label it as you will. Ejaculating is about making love, or making joy, or making babies, or just about the reduction of that sexual tension by whatever means possible... perhaps all of the above.

For most males, the ideal circumstance for satisfying the sexual urge is to be with a willing, receptive and aroused partner. The conscious goal is not the deposit of sperm, but rather the sharing of erotic pleasure. After what is hoped to be sufficient foreplay, possibly including an enthusiastic exchange of oral-genital stimulation, the main event occurs. Despite preferences, favorites, novelties and diversions, most heterosexual couples consummate their sexual encounters with genital intercourse.

There have been hundreds of books written over many centuries, each with the purpose of teaching a multitude of creative and, in some instances, contorted coital positions. Directed by some deep inner procreative road map, vaginal penetration seems to be a fairly simple act. However, the variety of arrangements by which two naked bodies accomplish this passionate copulatory act has been a topic of keen interest throughout our recorded history. Books on the multitude of coital positions clearly play to the human appeal for the recreational aspect of our sexuality. Indeed, sex should be fun, play should be novel and coital variety is wholeheartedly endorsed. The point, however, is that with all the enlightening words, illustrations, photos and explicit videos highlighting two bodies acrobatically entwined in coital harmony, the critical biological factor is that the penis has entered the vagina and pelvic thrusting has begun. Mother Nature has now become the man's co-pilot!! A program has been initiated that has started the neurological progression toward male ejaculation, with it's explosive release of the procreative semen.

I will now pose a critical question. Once penetration is accomplished, why does a man typically thrust in and out, rather than make circles or simply remain passive, allowing his penis to soak in the warmth of his partner's vagina? One answer is immediately apparent. Men thrust because it feels good! Another answer is less apparent. Men thrust because the most basic biological drive is not to do what feels good, but the instinct is to engage in that behavior that will trigger the deposit of the 80 million to 300 million sperm contained in each ejaculate. Thrusting, not soaking, leads to ejaculation. There would be very few pregnancies if the act of intercourse was confined to passive vaginal penetration with no additional movement. In fact, both procreation and recreation would suffer greatly in motionless sex, because it just so happens that the stimulation that moves a man to orgasm is the same stimulation that gives him the greatest pleasure! **Mother Nature intended it to work that way.**

If there is a natural drive to couple and a primitive urge to make vaginal penetration, and if this is built in, then I would argue that the thrusting mechanism is also hard-wired into our neurological system. Indeed, a great many people actually find "dirty dancing" to be very arousing... something about the gyrations of the hips and thighs taps into the body's sexual circuitry. The built in pelvic thrusting maneuver serves the biological function of moving the penis between the warm walls of the vagina and in this process exciting the nervous system to the point of the ejaculatory reflex... and it does feel awfully good along the way. It is my impression that thrusting brings erotic feelings directly to the penis (particularly around the head), but also indirectly through the involvement of the pelvic muscles. The biological program seems to read, "Get it up, get it in, get it moving, and get it off!" The psychological awareness is "This really feels great, I don't want to stop. I sure hope I don't come.... Oops!!"

In a more primitive jungle setting, rapid thrusting with a rapid ejaculation is a distinct advantage, because there is less vulnerability to attack by a predator. When survival is a concern and the primary motivation for sex is procreation, a quick ejaculation can be a lifesaver! Others have also speculated that rapid ejaculation is biologically rooted in the evolution of modern man. Bixer (1986) has entitled his article "Of Apes and Men (including Females)" and Hong (1984) cleverly calling is

"Survival of the Fastest." The male pelvis and penis seem to have been initially wired for a quick procreative act. A billion years ago, who would have ever imagined that there would someday be the safety and time for playful sexual recreation?

THE CHEMO/HYDRO/NEUROLOGICAL MECHANISM

It is difficult to write about ejaculation without putting the ejaculatory reflex into the context of the entire sexual response cycle. In thinking of our sexual response, we must first begin with the concept of sexual desire. This is the motivational aspect of male and female sexuality. Desire is the sex drive, historically called *libido*. It is our "horniness." When a male's sexual desire increases and he feels horny, he becomes restless, he may fantasize, and he might eventually begin the search for a satisfactory release. Sexual passion might motivate him to approach his spouse, proposition his girl friend, try his luck in a singles bar, purchase the services of a prostitute or, in the absence of a willing and responsive partner, to take matters into his own hand and masturbate. For most men, when desire becomes strong, a cold shower is not an acceptable alternative.

In pursuit of his satisfaction and with proper stimulation (both psychological and physical) the male's circulatory system increases blood flow into the three chambers of his penis (two along the top, one along the bottom). With the increase in his blood pressure and the increase in the volume of blood carried in by the arteries, the erectile tissue within his penis engorges and expands. The firmness of a man's erection is the result of this increased arterial blood flowing in and the closing off of the veins that would have otherwise carry the blood out. The greater the volume of blood trapped within the penile chambers, the harder the erection.

The erectile tissue and anatomical body of the penis actually begins within a man's body... it does not just hang on the outside! A urologist told a group of men, "I've got good news and I've got bad news. The good news is that your penis is twice as long as you think it is. The bad news is that half of it is inside!" As the penis engorges, leverage from within the body then lifts the firm penis to its erect state. The blood becomes trapped in the penis that has now become both hard and erect. In the absence of physical or psychological interference and with adequate stimulation, the erection will remain firm until an ejaculation has occurred.

As the sensitive nerve endings in the penis, especially those concentrated around the rim of the head (the *glans*), are stimulated, neurological energy begins to build. This is like cranking an electrical generator, building up the internal electrical charge. With the mechanical generator, a point is reached when the stored up electricity breaks out in the form of an arc. When a male's neuro/chemical energy builds to its threshold, a point is reached were this system is also going to pop... the ejaculatory discharge.

Now is as good a time as any to point out that the terms "e*jaculation*" and "*orgasm*" do not refer to the same function, although in most healthy neurologically-intact males they occur simultaneously. Ejaculation is the biological process by which the ejaculate (semen) is expelled through the urethral canal and out the end of the penis. Orgasm is the psychological experience of climactic pleasure associated with the physical release. There are some physical conditions (e.g., spinal cord injury) where an ejaculation can occur without the subjective experience of orgasm, and, conversely, a psychological orgasm is possible in the absence of the expulsion of semen. In this book the terms will be used interchangeable, as the two processes typically occur at the same moment.

It is also important at this time to point out that *ejaculation* is specifically the expulsion of the ejaculate that has collected at the very base or *bulb* of the penis (within the body). About 65% of the semen is fluid from the seminal vesicles, with about 30% coming from the prostate. This is the nourishing fluid for the sperm that are produced in the testicles. Despite the millions of sperm present, these carriers of genetic potential make up only about 5% of the total volume of the ejaculation. This is why a man will observe no perceptible change in the amount of his semen after a vasectomy.

There is an important process that precedes ejaculation known as *"emission."* If you think of it as "ignition" you will be close to the understanding of this as the priming of the ejaculatory cannon. Then, following a momentary delay, the gun is fired. It is during this emission phase that the ejaculatory load is moved from the seminal vesicles into the breech..into the prostate and base or *bulb* of the penis. As this happens, an internal "squish" is experienced by most men as the prostate contracts, and most men then know they have reached what Masters and Johnson have called the *"point of ejaculatory inevitability."* This is without question the point of no return... the trigger has been pulled and ejaculation is inevitable! Many partners know when their mates have reached this point of inevitability, as most guys find there is just enough time to mutter "Oh Shit!!"

It is the rhythmical contractions of the prostate, the *bulbocavernosus muscle* (that surrounds the urethral bulb), and other pelvic floor (*pubococcygeus*) muscles that send the ejaculate on its way through the urethra and out the end of the penis at an average exit velocity of 28 miles per hour. Simultaneous with these contractions are the waves of intense subjective pleasure that we have labeled the orgasm.

Most men, particularly as they age, lose penile firmness shortly after coming. The erection drops as the veins open up and carry blood back into the body. Despite a couple books claiming to help men learn how to become multiply orgasmic, there is no evidence that this can be accomplished and besides, most men are more interested in learning how to delay their first orgasm than in trying to learn how to come again. I think it unfortunate that there is yet another goal a man must reach. It's hard enough at times to slow things down... now we're supposed to be multiply orgasmic. Too much pressure!

Chapter 2

DEFINITIONS OF PREMATURE EJACULATION

THE PROFESSIONAL BOOKS

The Fourth Edition of the *Diagnostic and Statistical Manual (DSM-IV)*, official diagnostic "bible" for classifying mental health problems, describes premature ejaculation as "...the persistent or recurrent onset of orgasm and ejaculation with minimal sexual stimulation before, on, or shortly after penetration and before the person wishes it." It is classified as a mental health concern when it causes emotional distress or creates difficulties within a relationship.

In his highly acclaimed book, *The New Male Sexuality*, Bernie Zilbergeld states that "...the issue is really about voluntary control of the ejaculatory process rather than time." Dr. Zilbergeld continues, writing "The man lacks a vote or influence over when he comes. It happens when it happens, usually quickly and often seeming to sneak up on him."

Officially the label for inability to control is "premature ejaculation." The word "premature" means too early or before it is expected, as in a premature birth. The term premature ejaculation (abbreviated to "PE" by some writers) implies that the man's ejaculation was too early. One might wonder, when is too early and who decides?

Men may "unofficially" label themselves as having PE, while others with similar control are unconcerned. These subjective "self-diagnoses" are illustrated by the findings of Dr. Marilyn Safir (1997) of the University of Haifa in Israel. She and her colleagues found little difference in the duration of intercourse between those men who considered themselves normal and those who had applied for treatment of a sexual dysfunction.

Alfred Kinsey, in his 1948 report entitled the *Sexual Behavior of the Human Male* stated that in the study of 12,000 American men, three quarters reached orgasm within two minutes! Most men would say that two minutes is too early, and many women would agree. In a study of 1,000 couples published in 1966 (Gebhard) it was reported that the average duration of intercourse (from beginning to end but not necessarily with steady thrusting) lasted between 4 and 7 minutes.

These finding raise an interesting question. If 75% (75 out of 100) men, ejaculate in two to seven minutes, who is more typical... a man who lasts 15 minutes or one who lasts two?

Neither Kinsey nor Gebhard analyzed their findings in terms of how men thrust. Do rapid thrusters come more rapidly than casual thrusters? Neither did they analyze the data by position. Does a man in the "doggie position" ejaculate quicker than a man with his woman on top? Nor did the researchers inquire about frequency. Might we not imagine that a group of men having an ejaculation every other day will last longer, on average, than the men in a group who only come once in two weeks.

The Kinsey and Gebhard data on the one hand is of value, in that it reminds us that we are naturally quick comers, but on the other hand does not help us in the understanding of the reasons why some men are fast and others are not.

Another measure of coital success is the pleasure and results of intercourse from the female perspective. This was an attempt to get away from a stop-watch dependent definition. In this definition of premature ejaculation, it was stated that a man had PE if he ejaculated 50% of the time before his partner was able to orgasm. This definition was based on the assumption that women will always climax during intercourse if the man can last long enough.

It is bad logic to attempt to define male ejaculatory control in terms of his partner's ability to come with vaginal stimulation, as our best estimates tell us that only about 30 to 35% of all women have ever had an orgasm with intercourse, and our modern wisdom reminds us that for the majority of women it is stimulation of her clitoris, not her vagina, that is most likely to be her orgasmic trigger. Thus, with the majority of women, if we use her frequency of orgasm during intercourse as the measure of his control, the vast majority of men would be labeled premature ejaculators even if they were able to thrust for an hour.

THE MAN

Sex seems so natural. It just seems to happen. It should all unfold perfectly. As men, we experience that growing need for sexual satisfaction and are naturally drawn to an attractive and available partner. It should now work just like in the novels, where it begins with prolonged and passionate foreplay, moves through an easy transition into joyful penetration, followed by a medley of vigorous vaginal thrusts from a variety of directions, and culminating in simultaneous explosive orgasms after a half hour of mutual coital bliss. If this is our expectation, we will be very disappointed when reality does not match the fantasy and the entire event is over almost before it begins.

Men will argue, "But we should be able to last!" and "We should be able to ejaculate when we decide it is time!" Although, the surveys tell us that the average young male with steady thrusting will ejaculate within two to four minutes, men still seem to believe that they should automatically last an hour... and then come at will.

In my office men tell me of their embarrassment and their shame. "I felt terrible. She didn't say it, but I know she was disappointed." Even if a partner attempts to reassure her man, many guys will continue to beat themselves up. "She said it didn't matter to her, but I know I'll lose her if I can't last longer." Even when I suggest that there are other ways to satisfy a woman (oral or manual), and even when the partner agrees, men will often hang onto the belief that the only way to please a woman is with steady and prolonged vaginal thrusting. The end result is that the man feels inadequate, insecure about his ability to please, and fearful that his partner will go out looking for that guy who can last an hour. The sense of failure can be great and, in most instances, the man becomes a worse critic of his performance than is his partner.

Fear and apprehension begin to accumulate around sexual performance. With all this anxiety, married men and men in committed relationships often begin avoiding sexual encounters, leading their partners to worry they are no longer attractive. If feeling anxious, single men may end relationships before they can become sexual, or stop dating all together, not wanting to be placed in the awkward situation of having to deal with another disappointing encounter. As we will see, avoidance and anxiety are counterproductive and may actually perpetuate the problem.

THE PARTNER

Many women do not seem to understand the near-automatic process involved in a man reaching orgasm. Believing that every man should have total ejaculatory control, these women are likely to feel cheated and over time to develop strong feelings of resentment. These feelings are likely to be even more intense if the woman believes that she can only orgasm with the prolonged stimulation of vaginal intercourse. If she has never experienced an orgasm, she is likely to blame her male companion's rapid ejaculation for this and to hold him responsible for cheating her out of her fulfillment. Believing that he should have complete control, she may see him as selfish and as only interested in his own gratification. When this is expressed to her partner, he is likely to feel even more guilt, intensifying his feeling of pressure to perform.

It is also surprising how many women firmly believe that love and ejaculatory control are somehow related. Such women will be heard proclaiming, "If he loved me, he would wait!" For her, the rapid ejaculation becomes a sign that her partner really is uncaring. It may not matter that he has been quick with every partner in the past, for her his quickness is a very personal thing that she unjustly uses as her barometer of his love. "I know that if you really love me you'll wait!" How's that for pressure?

Since many other women wholeheartedly enjoy all the pleasures of foreplay and are orgasmic in many different ways, these women might feel badly only because their man feels badly. She feels sorry for him. She's disappointed that he was disappointed. Typically the message "I enjoyed all that there was but I feel badly for you" is heard by the man as "I'll lie to try to make you feel better and it really was terrible for me." Men need to listen more carefully to these women and to believe that for some women, although pleasant, prolonged intercourse is not what it is all about.

At times it happens that a couple will begin their encounter with quiet words and loving touch. The sexual caress will be pleasant and the emotional closeness terrific. The man will pleasure his partner with his hands and his tongue, possibly even bringing her to orgasm more than once. Then, after all this wonderful time together the man will mount, insert, stroke twice and come! If he becomes angry with himself and "bent out of shape," he might abruptly pull away from his partner, turn his back on her and brood. She then feels cut off, devalued and abandoned... not a very nice ending to what for her had begun as a very pleasant experience. Despite all the good feelings she had experienced, at this point she is likely to promise herself that it will be a long time before setting herself up for that same painful ending. It is amazing how easily a good experience can retroactively be turned into a disaster. I will talk later about focusing on the *joyful process*, rather than fretting over the *final outcome*. Stop ruining an otherwise wonderful experience just because you got carried away... it's not your fault... **Mother Nature made you do it!**

THE COUPLE

By now it should be clear that I believe the surveys and I believe the hundreds of women with whom I have spoken. The majority of women are <u>not</u> orgasmic during intercourse and most women will orgasm more reliably with direct clitoral stimulation provided by fanciful fingers, a talented tongue or favorite vibrator. Informal surveys suggest, in fact, that the majority of women would choose *cunnilingus* (oral stimulation of their genitals) over vaginal intercourse if they had to choose just one. Cunnilingus is such a valuable gift for a man to give that I have written an entire book on the loving art of orally satisfying a woman (Birch, 1996).

If a woman enjoys everything and is orgasmic in many ways, she is less likely to view intercourse as the exclusive source of her pleasure. If her partner is understanding of her versatility and finds joy in giving her joy, there is less pressure on him to perform long and well with intercourse. With these couples there is no self-punitive reaction on the part of the rapid ejaculator and the woman is not disappointed that the intercourse was brief. These couples do not collectively and retroactively damage the pre-coital fun they had shared. It is as if she had her turn (and he very much enjoyed his role as the giver of her pleasure) and now it is his turn. Although his turn is relatively brief, she had fun, he had fun and after his orgasm they snuggle, complimenting each other on a job well done. Within such a relationship, should we label him a premature ejaculator? I would argue that premature ejaculation is as much a definition determined by the couple as it is by the sexological "experts."

If the definition is really relative, depending in part on the woman's versatility and her perception of intercourse, one would imagine that what worked for the man in one relationship might not work in another. In fact, in my practice I have seen many examples of a man, who within one long extended relationship was never labeled quick by himself or partner, but upon entering another relationship is immediately confronted by a woman who chastises him for not waiting! While there are such relationships within which rapidness of ejaculation is not an issue, many rapid ejaculators are in relationships where it does indeed create distress.

I do not mean to cast blame on the partner nor to imply that every woman should devalue intercourse and settle for what she can get. There is great variety in what women prefer, respond to, appreciate and value. The desires of a woman can not be demeaned or ignored. As an equal partner in the encounter, she does have the right to seek what is most pleasurable and meaningful to her. Thus, I will not write rapid ejaculation off as a biologically necessity nor attempt to persuade women that intercourse need not be prolonged. Obviously, for a multitude of physical and emotional reasons, the majority of both men and women do value the genital intimacy of intercourse, do experience physical pleasure with that coupling, and do value spending a reasonable amount of time entwined in that coital embrace. Most premature

DEFINITIONS OF PREMATURE EJACULATION

ejaculators would like to learn ejaculatory control... and their partners would like them to do so as well.

Let me share a few words of wisdom at this point. Literally, "You can't screw a relationship together!" If there are relationship problems, the non-sexual issues need to be attended to first. A cooperative and responsive partner is required for effective learning. Thus it is quite difficult to work on premature ejaculation when a relationship is in trouble.

RAPID OR PREMATURE?

Up to this point I have used the terms "*rapid ejaculation*" and "*premature ejaculation*" interchangeably. Various writers seem to prefer one term over the other and, quite honestly, I would rather talk of a man being rapid than of him being premature. The connotation is somehow different in my mind, with *premature* implying something more pathological or problematic. *Rapid* is simply a description. Consider a foot race were all the runners are poised at the starting line. It is quite a different thing if the announcer states "Bill Jones started rapidly," as compared with "Bill Jones started prematurely." It is OK to have started rapidly, but not to have jumped the gun prematurely! *Early ejaculation* is another term you might encounter. I wonder, if there is early ejaculation, when does it become late?

24 - Male Sexual Endurance

I will, with some reluctance, give in to the "official" label "premature ejaculation," conceding that most rapid ejaculators feel they did indeed come prematurely... coming before they or their partner wanted it to happen. I will, therefore, continue to switch back and forth, but always mindful of the belief that this condition is more natural than pathological.

THE RAPID EJACULATORS

It is now pretty much accepted in the field of sexology that there is not just one expression of rapid ejaculation. Rapid ejaculators present a variety of histories and give very different descriptions of their perceived problem.

It would come as no surprise to hear a young man tell of his prolonged masturbation, but when tested by an exciting new partner, he tells of being totally out of control. Quite often these fellows settle down as the relationship progresses and, if they can keep from worrying, their control improves with time. However, these men upon leaving a relationship in which their endurance had improved, initially re-experience the loss of control with each new partner. Note three important considerations. First, the man is young. The second important piece of information is that he feels he could, when alone, last forever with self stimulation. Finally, he can identify the combined excitement and anxiety of a new and novel encounter, but can recall that he becomes more controlled as the novelty wears off and as his relaxation improves. These men are not likely to seek professional help and, over time, they fall into a long-term stable relationship and do quite well.

It will also happen that a man will experience greater endurance when he has ample sexual opportunities and is ejaculating frequently. When the number of ejaculations decrease, his control seems to be lost. I have seen this typically in situations where a college couple will meet over the summer, quickly developing a passionate and loving relationship. Sexual encounters are frequent and of good duration. When fall arrives and each head off to different colleges, they must limit their time together to just two weekends per month. Any semblance of control is gone!

Another man may relate that he does quite well, lasting a significant amount of time and feeling under good control with one woman, but with a second woman in his life he unavoidably ejaculates rapidly each and every time. He can offer no information about masturbation, as between his two lovers he has no time nor need for self pleasuring. Typically the man will identify something unique about the woman with whom he ejaculates rapidly, quite often this being that she is more highly aroused and passionate than his other lover. Although quick, he describes these intimate encounters as much more exciting... there is good news and bad... "It is fantastic, but I come immediately!"

Then there is the middle-aged man who says he has always been able to prolong his masturbation, and is not quick to come with oral stimulation. However, despite the long-term nature of his relationship he still ejaculates rapidly each and every time he attempts intercourse. He states that he will come within a minute... two minutes at best.

Another man of about the same age complains that he is quick each and every time with masturbation, oral sex and intercourse. However, he is occasionally able to obtain a second erection and when this happens he is able to thrust for a good amount of time before his second ejaculation (if there is one to be had). He has always been quick, regardless of the stimulation and, as a younger man, always counted on his second erections to last longer. As he ages, however, his ability to become aroused a second time has become much less predictable.

One more man now recalls how he has always been quick with every kind of stimulation, at times ejaculating while pleasuring his partner without even being touched. He says that he reliably gets not just a second, but a third erection each and every time. His second ejaculation is just as quick as the first and his third takes only slightly longer. I am no longer surprised when some of these men also report that they are still having *nocturnal emissions* ("wet dreams") although most of us stopped having these by the age of sixteen. This is most dramatic when the man is in his fifth decade of life when the majority of his peers are slowing down both in speed and in frequency.

It becomes obvious that rapid ejaculation may be a condition only during youth or only with early encounters with new partners. It may happen when ejaculations are sparse, but not when plentiful. It can also be a lifelong condition and occur with every encounter, regardless of the stimulation, the duration of the relationship or the frequency of ejaculation.

There is, however, one more variation in which a man reports a long history of good control and then, later in life, seems to have lost this ability to last and begins to climax even faster than when in his youth! When this happens with an older man, there is the question of decreased frequency... is he coming faster now because his sexual encounters occur less often? Are there relationship problems causing the couple to back away from each other and "make love" less frequently? Is there also increased stress in his life at this time? Stress and anxiety may be involved both in problems of getting or keeping an erection and in unexpected loss of control. It is not surprising then to hear an older man (under stress) report at times he is not getting good erections, and when he does he is ejaculating quickly?

Regardless of how rapid ejaculation presents itself, as an old concern or a new one, specific to a partner or with everyone, there is likely to be personal distress and the relationship may begin to suffer. Society projects the expectation that men should last forever. As we know, however, not every man can, and at times it seems the harder he tries, the worse it gets!

Chapter 3

THE MYTH
OF PERFECT CONTROL

THE CONTEST

We have grown up in a competitive society where achievement has been assigned high value. There are those who strive for academic achievement, while the more athletic do it on the playing field, and the entrepreneurial do it in the stock market. There are dance contests, beauty contests, singing contests, and talent contests to find out who is tops at just about everything. We have been socialized to do our best... "Anything worth doing is worth doing well!" Who has the best dog or the best horse? Who has put up the most lights at Christmas time? There is a lot of pressure to do well, and there are rewards for doing so.

No complaints... this is what encourages free enterprise, makes our economy work and allows people to discover their excellence. However, in this competitive atmosphere how can we not help but wish to be an expert lover, to give the best pleasure, and to trigger our partner's strongest orgasms. We would love to win the coveted "sexpert's" trophy and crave to be remembered for "a job well done." Why not, we have been socialized to try to be the best at everything else... and if we can't be, at least we ought to be good in bed!

THE RESPONSE

In our complex technological society, we receive detailed instructions (often in three languages) on how to properly operate a new VCR! Almost every household in America has at least one video cassette recorder, along with that detailed operational manual. However, when we men received our most personal equipment we were not given a book of instructions! After all, we didn't need one for our lungs!!

We need make no effort to trigger a heart beat and healthy lungs fill with air without conscious effort. Our kidneys know what to do and there is no need to instruct our stomach on the fine art of digesting food. Our waste disposal system also runs pretty much on it's own... well, pretty much so, for at some time in our early years we did need to learn to control not "the how," but "the when!"

As adults, having perfected it, we take our bowl and bladder control for granted, assuming that it works as automatically as our other physical systems. We also seem to take our ejaculatory control for granted, assuming that perfection should naturally be there also.

The myth of perfect control is spawned by the belief that Mother Nature designed sex to last and no instructional manual is required. The myth is fuel by the desire to be the best in a competitive world where it seems that every other man can last forever. **Sexuality is perfectly natural but, unfortunately, it is not naturally perfect!**

THE JOKES

We must consider how a sensitive man with rapid ejaculation must feel every time a joke is told about coming too fast. Since men often cling to the myth of perfect and effortless control and will only swap their stories of phenomenal performance, the rapid ejaculator might believe that he belongs to a very small minority. Premature ejaculation becomes his closely guarded secret and when the jokes are told, the "minute man" must hide his shame. Years ago, comedian Joan Rivers, appearing on the Tonight Show, quipped something like, "I stopped dating younger men. I got tired of that game they play... you know, 1, 2, 3... ready or not here I come!" Everyone laughed. If it had been a joke about color, one could protest, saying "I am of that color and I resent that cruel and insensitive joke." However, it would be hard to imagine a man saying to a group, "I am a premature ejaculator and I am deeply hurt by what you said!"

Books, movies and TV joke about the rapid ejaculator while the more serious romantic episodes portray men as being under perfect control. Even more devastating to the rapid ejaculator's ego are the adult videos in which prolonged rapid pile-driving thrusting is routine... and did you see the size of that thing?

It is interesting that the sayings that have evolved to reassure the man worried about size, emphasize stay power as more important than the dimensions of his equipment. "It's not the size of the plow that matters, but how long you can keep it in the ground!" Ouch! Now guys are not only going to worry about the length of their penis, they are also going to worry about the length of their endurance! If we are not careful with what we teach, teenage boys will measure themselves not only with a ruler, but with a stop watch as well!

THE SEXUAL RESPONSE CYCLE

Within an erotic encounter, there is a sequence of feelings and events that sex therapists refer to as the *sexual response cycle*. It begins with desire (the motivational aspect or drive of our sexuality) and, with mental and/or physical stimulation, leads to arousal or excitement. With continued stimulation a plateau of arousal is achieved, and as the stimulation continues and the neurological and psychological energies build, the *point of ejaculatory inevitability* is reached. Very shortly thereafter the ejaculation/orgasm occurs.

Simply put, the cycle begins with a feeling of horniness and, if there is stimulation between a man's ears and/or between his legs, blood is packed into his penis. The result is the firming and elevation of that organ, now more sensitive to touch than in its flaccid state. Physical stimulation of this erection moves a man to a high and very pleasant state of awareness which eventually (and inevitably) pushes him over the brink... and he comes. As can be seen on the following graphs, the difference between a man with ejaculatory control and a rapid ejaculator is the speed with which men move from one stage of the cycle to the next. The premature ejaculator speeds through the arousal, almost skips the plateau and is often caught by surprise as he suddenly finds himself at the point of no return. It is amazing how quickly time flies when you are having fun!!

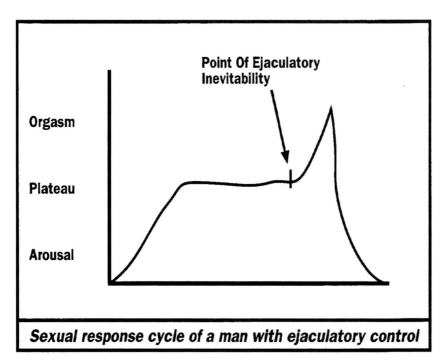

Sexual response cycle of a man with ejaculatory control

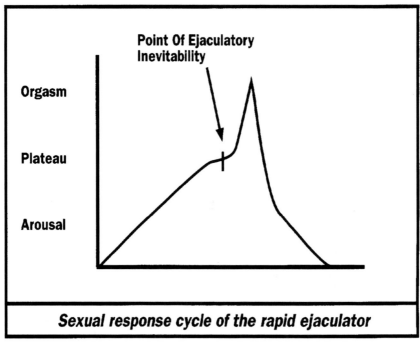

Sexual response cycle of the rapid ejaculator

The ability to slow the process does not come naturally (not in Ma Nature's original plan) and some men are apparently unable to develop control easily. We also know that even those with apparent control are not perfect in their management of their ejaculatory reflex, at times being surprised by an unintentional slip. In learning ejaculatory control, a man must learn to slow his assent up the ladder of excitement and linger a bit longer within the pleasant plateau of arousal. It will not be a perfect control and it will not always be easily won.

HOPING FOR A SECOND CHANCE

Just as there seems to be a wide range of levels of sexual desire and great variability among men in terms of sensitivity and control, there are differences between men when it comes to the length of time it takes to obtain a second ejaculation. As a general rule, it takes less time to achieve a second erection than it does to come a second time. In other words, some men can get it up again within a relatively brief period of time, but can not ejaculate with that second erection... but others can.

A second general rule is that the time between the ejaculations of young men is briefer than that among older guys... but this is not always true. A third generalization is that the more exciting the partner, the more likely it is that a second ejaculation will occur within a brief period of time... but not always so.

Another general rule is that the man with a higher sex drive is more likely to possess the potential for a second ejaculation... although this is not automatically the case. Finally, the longer it has been since the last ejaculation in a past encounter (with a partner or with masturbation) and the first one in the present erotic episode, the greater the chances for a repeat performance. Saved up sexual energy might just afford the man an occasional encore... although there is a point of diminishing returns. The "use it or lose it" principle also applies, particularly for the aging male. By the time a man reaches into his firth or sixth decade of life, waiting too long may create a problem of coming too fast without the benefit of a second chance or, worse yet, difficulty in achieving even the first erection.

In summary, the man most likely to have a second erection and ejaculation is a very horny young man who has not had a sexual outlet in weeks and is now with an exciting and responsive new partner. As his level of desire drops, so does his potential. As he ages, second chances become less available. If he is having frequent sex with a familiar partner there may be very little hope for a second ejaculation within the same encounter and indeed, for whatever reason or reasons, most men must wait to recharge their batteries and reload their guns!

The time between ejaculations is know as the *refractory period*, and this "down time" is influenced by many factors... including those mentioned above. However, physical health, certain medications, level of stress or fatigue, general mood, and quality of the relationship are but a few other variables that will stretch out that refractory period... hours, days, or sometimes weeks.

The refractory period is typically independent of the ability to control ejaculation. If there is justice in life, one would think that the premature ejaculator should at least be entitled to a second try. Not so, as those men who can bounce back quickly for a second round might be rapid ejaculators or might be men with perfect control. I think a brief refractory period and the ability to ejaculate twice in one encounter has a lot to do with a man's basic wiring. I do not think this ability can be learned. Therefore, I do not advise wasting money on those books that promise to teach men how to become multiply orgasmic. Let's leave that skill to some lucky women, and **work on getting it right the first time.**

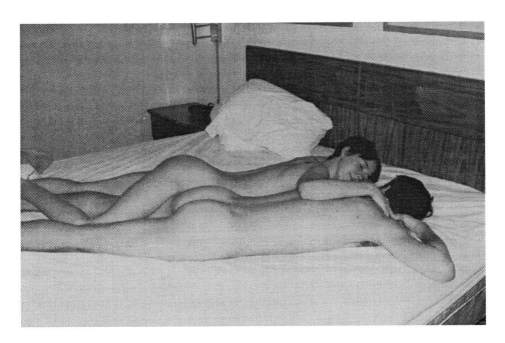

Chapter 4

IN PURSUIT OF A CURE

THE JELLS AND CREAMS

Open any adult toy catalog or search the shelves of any adult novelty store and you will find a variety of jells and creams that promise nonstop action. Among these products you will find such names as "Maintain," "Retain," and "Sustain," reflecting both the promise and an active ingredient such as **benzocaine** or **xylocaine**. These and similar chemicals are topical anesthetics and are the active ingredient in many other over-the-counter creams that are designed to numb superficial nerve endings to relieve a pain or to soothe an itch. Solarcaine, for example, is sold to relieve the discomfort of sun burn, while Americaine will lessen the pain from a minor cut. Repackaged and renamed, similar products find a ready market among men with ejaculatory concerns.

The man buying a desensitizing cream apparently assumes that by chemically numbing the surface of his penis, he can prolong intercourse. One product containing benzocaine is also cherry flavored, which must imply that it will also allow the man to maintain control while receiving oral stimulation (*fellatio*).

There are many problems with the use of these creams. If it is true that the penis of the premature ejaculator has superficial nerves that are hypersensitive, the first question centers on the amount of cream to use and when to apply it. Too little too late might be ineffective, while too much too soon might create an anesthetized member that feels nothing.

The next concern revolves around the fact that anything that will desensitize a man's penis will just as easily desensitize the tender tissue of a woman's genitals. A flavored cream is ridiculous, as most women are understandably unwilling to sacrifice having feeling in their lips and tongue just to give a partner prolonged head. If the goal is prolonged mutual pleasure, but both partner's are numb, isn't the purpose defeated? The man could, of course, apply the cream and then pull a condom over his penis, but unless a condom is required for safe sex and/or contraception, some spontaneity will be lost in all this preparation.

My major concern about such products is that there is no evidence that these unreasonably expensive creams and jells really work! I do not, therefore, recommend their use. Its is not clear to what extent the superficial nerves are involved in the ejaculatory process and there is no research showing that simply numbing of these surface nerves is effective. Furthermore, in relying on these products, the man neglects the more important challenge which is to learn a natural non-chemical means of ejaculatory control.

CONDOMS

Long before the process for curing rubber was discovered, condoms were fashioned from the intestines of sheep. These sheaths of animal gut were fitted with a draw string that, when tied, held these early condoms in place. Given the rarity and expense of the forerunners of latex "rubbers," the gut condoms were recycled, being meticulously washed, thoroughly dried, and carefully stored after each use. Written instructions also became available to housewives, explaining how they could purchase raw animal intestine at the local butcher shop and then process these entrails for use as a condom. Called "naturals" or "skins," condoms of animal membrane can still be found, but they tend to be expensive. Additionally, these condoms, unlike their latex counterparts, do not provide protection from HIV, the AIDS virus.

By the second half of the 1800s, thick uncomfortable rubber condoms began to appear. However, it was not until 1884 that Charles Goodyear patented his process for "vulcanizing" rubber... the real business of mass producing latex condoms could now begin. In the 1920s the Youngs Rubber

Company began production of it's latex condom and began marketing their "Trojans" through drug stores... "for the prevention of disease." The greatest need for a reliable condom, of course, was for birth control (still a dirty word back then) and by the 1930s, one and a half million condoms were being sold daily!

Hoag Levins, in his fascinating book *American Sex Machines*, looks at the history of sex through the records of the U.S. Patent Office. A search of government records has revealed that over the years, condoms of a wide variety of shapes, sizes and configurations have been patented. Recognizing the concern with rapid ejaculation, a patent was granted in 1950 for the design of what was claimed to be a sensation-deadening condom. This rubber looked much like a typical condom, except the end covering the head of the penis was quite thick. In 1957 another inventor argued that it was unnecessary to deny sensation to the entire head (*glans*), and patented a design for a condom that he believed would delay ejaculation. When applied correctly, this condom would have had a thickened area on the underside of the penis, covering the sensitive *frenulum*. The sensation barrier was to be twelve times as think as the surrounding rubber membrane.

The production and sale of sensation-deadening condoms of one design or another is not widespread. Indeed, the condom industry seems dedicated to the production of stronger but thinner condoms. Even with the emphasis on super thin latex and super sensitivity for the wearer, many men complain about having to wear a condom.

We'll all heard (and maybe even stated) that "wearing a condom is like taking a shower in a raincoat," or "like trying to feel velvet while wearing a glove!" If men complain about feeling less sensation while wearing a condom, wouldn't it then follow that wearing a condom would slow down a rapid ejaculator?

I have talked with men who have wisely begun their new sexual relationships wearing a condom for both protection and contraception, but as trust grew and a decision was made for the woman to "go on the pill," these guys suddenly discovered that they had no ejaculatory control. Making penetration without that layer of latex proved to be too exciting. Some men eventually settled down, but others did not.

Over the years I have heard a mixture of reports on the use of condoms. Some men who would come at the drop of a hat without a condom could not ejaculate at all when suited up in their raincoat. Others claimed that they had no trouble ejaculating, but did seem to last a bit longer when their penis was covered with latex. Still others reported no difference at all. A few men have even complained that they rarely had an opportunity to try a condom during intercourse, as they would ejaculating while rolling the rubber down over their erection!

A man's subjective reaction to wearing a condom might be dependent, in some small part, on the presence or absence of a lubricant. Remember, lubricated condoms have as much lubrication on the <u>inside</u> as they do on the outside. With lubrication present between the latex sheath and the erection, the man's penis may slide a bit within the condom... giving subjective feelings of slipperiness and the impression of a greater awareness of the partner's wetness. It would be my guess, therefore, that some rapid ejaculators would last longer wearing a dry condom than wearing one that is lubricated.

Condoms are an absolute necessity in the practice of **safer sex** and are quite effective in the preventing of the transmission of many of the sexually transmitted diseases. When used properly, they are also an effective means of birth control. Condoms are a bit more effective when lubricated, given that most lubricants contain a spermicide (usually **Nonoxynol-9**) that will kill both sperm and a variety of viruses. Thus, **there are several good reasons for using a condom quite independent of the issue of ejaculatory control.** When a condom needs to be used, it needs to be used! The consequences of not using one when you should may create misery that will last considerably longer than the after glow from a hot sexual encounter.

In a safe committed relationship and with no concerns about contraception, wearing a condom to delay ejaculation may be an unreliable or unsatisfactory remedy. Some women, when they feel safe, would prefer intercourse without a condom and, of course, so would the majority of men. Given the unpredictability of the condom as a solution to rapid ejaculation, I highly recommend our latex friends for safety and for birth control, but urge the rapid ejaculator to learn a more natural means of control.

THE STRAPS

Latex and velcro® straps are now being sold for ejaculatory control. Based on the observation that a man's scrotum pulls up tightly against his body as he becomes aroused and that his testicles rotate slightly just prior to ejaculation, some clever soul devised a strap to be placed around the top of the scrotal sac above the testicles that hang below. This strap must be put in place before arousal, before the scrotum begins to thicken and shrink up close to the body. Thus it must be in place prior to excitement and the resulting erection. The assumption seems to be that preventing the natural elevation of the testicles during high level stimulation will, in some mechanical way, delay the ejaculation.

The assumption might be faulty, but this is a relatively new product and "the jury is still out." I have seen no research on the effectiveness of such straps, although I would imagine that they could be cumbersome during foreplay and might be distracting to both the man and his partner during intercourse. If they work at all, it might well be because they are uncomfortable to wear and therefore distracting, causing the man to focus more on the tight strap around his scrotum than on his sexual pleasure.

THE PILLS

It had been found that some medications (most notably among the antidepressants) sometimes inhibit orgasm **as a side effect**. That is, when Paxil, for example, has been prescribed for a man as treatment for depression, he hopefully reports the main effect of a happier mood. However, he might also report a side effect of delayed ejaculation. Physicians have long wanted to lay claim to the ability to "cure" sexual problems through medical intervention, so this unexpected side effect caught their attention. Medical practitioners reasoned that men who were not depressed but were rapid ejaculators might be slowed down by the same medication. It has, in fact, helped a small percentage of premature ejaculators, but, as a non-physician, I worry about the wisdom of taking a drug for its side effect! And, I would ask, for how long would the physicians expect men to be using this medication? Since rapid ejaculation can be a life-long concern, are men hopelessly dependent on medication for ejaculatory control?

There is a more positive side to the issue of medical control. If loss of sexual confidence is a factor and anxiety is a component of the lack of ejaculatory control, **relatively brief** use of a medication could allow the man to gain confidence in his sexual abilities. This could then in turn result in a reduction of his performance anxiety. There is some chance, therefore, that he will continue to do well after he has ceased using the drug. However, I do worry about this search for a quick pharmacologic fix in place of learning a non-chemical (behavioral) method of control. Despite brief improvement while on the medication, if the man did not understand what had happened between his ears, the problem between his legs will return!

CONSTRICTION BANDS

It is relatively safe to trap blood in an erect penis for up to half an hour. *Cock rings* or *love rings* of various designs have a long history, believed to date back to ancient China, then spreading quickly among the Japanese. Rings of metal, ivory, jade, wood, and many other materials have been placed around the base of a penis (or under the scrotum and around the penis) in this ageless attempt to make erections harder and keep them longer. More recently, the use of a tight rubber constriction band around the base of the penis has been shown to be a practical (mechanical) alternative for the man who gets an erection but loses his firmness before penetration and before he can ejaculate. If a band or ring will prevent a man from losing an erection **before** he ejaculates, it will also prevent the loss of it **after** he comes.

Many men who are unable to control the timing of their ejaculation and subsequently lose their erections immediately after coming, have used a cock ring or constriction band to at least preserve their firmness after their own climax. The thinking must be, in part, that the partner can continue to enjoy the prolonged thrusting, even if the man in his post-orgasmic state has lost erotic sensation in his penis. This mechanical maintenance might be important for women who are only orgasmic with intercourse and would have been denied climax if the erection had fallen away. However, for those women who are not reliably orgasmic during intercourse or are orgasmic in a variety of different ways, something might get lost in her passion when she becomes aware that her partner has passed his peak experience and is now mechanically pumping her with a numb penis because he believes this is what she wants... or to satisfy a male ego that demands he prolong intercourse at any cost!

In order to retain blood in an erection, the band must be relatively tight. There is a problem, however, in getting a tight constriction band in place at the base of an erect penis. Many men have attempted to roll a rubber band down the length of their shaft, snagging pubic hairs and pinching tender skin in the process... and then there is the problem of getting it off once finished!

In fairness to the use of the bands, I should point out that it is possible to buy a simple rigid plastic ring around which the elastic rubber constriction band is placed. The larger rigid ring is then dropped down over the erect penis and the band pushed off around its base. With the band now in place, the plastic ring is removed.

Commercial rubber constriction bands are made with tabs that can be gripped and pulled when ready to stop, stretching the band away from the penis and allowing blood to flow out and the erection to drop. The rubber constriction band is then easily slid from the soft member. One problem with obtaining the rigid plastic applicator ring and the well designed easily-removable elastic bands is that these are sold as "medical supplies" and, as such, are greatly over-priced and available only on a physician's prescription.

The issue of discomfort must also be addressed, for as noted, in order to be effective the bands must be tight. Many men lose their enthusiasm for this simple solution when they experience the discomfort of a tight band at the base of their penis. The band might also cause discomfort for the woman, particularly if during intercourse she has enjoyed being on top, staying in close and rubbing her clitoris against the base of her partner's penis. Something new will be there and she must now contend with a foreign object in what had been her favorite rubbing area. However, some women may find that the rubber band is not unfriendly and have manage to work with it, or around it.

Finally, when a constriction band is placed around the base of the penis and is tight enough to restrict blood, it will also be tight enough to restrict the flow of the ejaculate. In other words, the wearer is likely to experience a *retrograde ejaculation*. This means that the ejaculate fluid that has moved down from the seminal vesicles and prostate can not be expelled out the end of the penis upon orgasm. The passageway (the urethra) has been blocked and the forceful orgasmic contractions will drive the ejaculate back up through the prostate and into the bladder. Nothing will exit the penis, as the semen will now back up and mix with the man's urine. There will be a new sensation as the seminal fluid passes back through the prostate (a sharp pain for some). Structural damage to "the plumbing" is unlikely and the ejaculate, now mixed with urine, will be "peed" away the next time the man urinates. There will be no wet spot on the sheets to contend with, but at the cost of the man losing the sensation of ejaculate traveling the length of his penis and at the risk of experiencing brief momentary pain. For some, the intensity of the orgasmic explosion might mask any discomfort, but for others the discomfort will definitely detract from their pleasure.

It is hoped that the reader appreciates my belief that there are no quick fixes and that mechanical and medical options are not without significant drawbacks.

THE DOCTORS

Over 25 years ago, Masters & Johnson (1970) optimistically predicted that premature ejaculation could "...be brought fully under control in our culture during the next decade." Now two and a half decades after that prediction was made, concerns over rapid ejaculation remain the number one sexual complaint among young men and certainly a significant concern among all men regardless of age. Some writers have estimated that between 30 and 75% of men think of themselves as coming too soon. Even with a more conservative estimate of 29% reported in *The Social Organization of Sexuality* (1994), rapid ejaculation remains the number one sexual complaint among men.

Rouleau (1980), writing in a professional journal in Belgium, identified premature ejaculation as a problem, but then offered the assurance that "...fortunately, PE is easily treated with short term therapy." Helen Singer Kaplan, M.D., Ph.D., in her 1989 book entitled PE: How to *Overcome Premature Ejaculation*, claims that "...over 90 percent of premature ejaculators can be cured within an average of 14 weeks of treatment." There again is that troublesome concept of "cure," with no acknowledgment of the finding that within a three year period most men lose whatever gains had been made.

Bernie Zilbergeld, Ph.D., in his 1992 book, *The New Male Sexuality*, says "While ejaculation is a reflex and can't be controlled perfectly, a man who has developed control can enjoy high levels of sexual arousal, whether from oral or manual stimulation or intercourse, without coming, and he usually has a choice when to ejaculate" Later he writes, "Lack of ejaculatory control isn't a bad problem to have, because sex therapists have been very successful in resolving it." Once more we see rapid ejaculation presented as a "problem" (albeit not a "bad" one), with the inference being that the normal or natural state is one of control and once the problem is "resolved" the man returns to the norm.

I would argue that rapid ejaculation is itself the norm, but ejaculatory control (or at least management) can be learned. It should be remembered that the "official psychiatric bible," the *Diagnostic and Statistical Manual*, cautions us to only consider it a mental health problem when it causes emotional distress or creates difficulties within a relationship. When there is distress, is the real problem the rapid ejaculation, or is it the unrealistic expectations of how long a man really should last and how much control he should naturally have? Obviously it is some of both, as a man coming rapidly in a society that advocates marathon copulation is likely to be in trouble with himself and prove to be troublesome within his relationship.

Dr. Zilbergeld goes on to say "According to a number of studies and clinical impressions, 80 to 90 percent of men learn better control in therapy, provided they are willing to devote the necessary time and energy." He estimates that ejaculatory control can be learned in eight to twelve weeks. I am uncomfortable with his implication that better control can only be learned with therapy, as I believe that the vast majority of men master ejaculatory control without professional help. I am also uncomfortable with predicting a definite time within which improvement should occur... Dr. Kaplan had said fourteen weeks, Dr. Zilbergeld said eight to twelve.

Suggesting a time frame adds additional pressure and another expectation. The pressure is to beat the clock (must be something terribly wrong if it takes longer to fix) and the expectation is that once complete, the "cure" will last forever. Masters and Johnson had predicted that premature ejaculation could "...be brought fully under control in our society..." and thought that this should have happened fifteen years ago. We wouldn't have to be talking about all of this if they had been right!

It is understandable that rapid ejaculation was misunderstood in the 1970s when so little was really known of the human sexual response. However, it is distressing to me to find contemporary literature, supposedly written by medical experts, that reflects a total ignorance of the process for managing premature ejaculation. A prime example is found in the Sixth Edition of *Take Care of Yourself* (1996) by Donald Vickery, M.D. and James Fries, M.D. Billed as "The Complete Illustrate Guide to Medical Self-Care" the book cover proclaims "More Than 10,000,000 Copies Sold." The doctors do correctly identify anxiety as being involved in the problem of premature ejaculation, but simply suggest that "...relaxation is usually a solution." Sounds so very easy! They go on to offer ... "other potential aids."

The doctors Vickery and Fries state briefly but confidently that "A firm pinch on the tip of the penis will delay ejaculation. A condom usually decreases sensation so that ejaculation is delayed. Seldom are such measures necessary for more than a few occasions." That's it!! I certainly hope these medical practitioners have done a better job elsewhere in the book in their descriptions of how to deal with snake bites and nose bleeds!

Dr. Derek Polonsky, in the video entitled *You Can Last Longer* notes that "...few men can have complete control over when they ejaculate. From time to time almost any man can be taken by surprise and come before he intended to."

Therapist Pauline Abrams, in a 1979 article appearing in *Forum,* wrote "Many men think that after their problem of rapid ejaculation is solved they will be able to thrust like a speedy jackhammer for lengthy periods of time." I wonder who told them they should be able to pound away for hours on end? The myth continues! **How have we allowed ourselves to believe this and, if we have known better, why haven't we taught our sons otherwise?**

Rapid ejaculation is not a pathological condition, curable within a set time frame and then forgotten about. I believe it to be a normal variation that can be managed, but what must be learned is an approach that requires close attention until age naturally slows the man down... if it ever does. Don't become discouraged and quit reading. Your sexuality will remain fun, and, as you learn more about ejaculatory control, you will be learning to communicate even better and learning more about your partner's preferences and pleasures. If you have read other self-help manuals for rapid ejaculators, **you will find something different here... not so much in what I tell you to do with the machinery between your legs, but more in terms of what I tell you to do with that computer between your ears! While I may not fully explain** *why* **you are quick, I will try to show you** *how* **to manage your response.**

Chapter 5

THE SEARCH FOR A REASON

THE ASSUMPTION

We seem to believe that by understanding the reason for something, it will go away. However, understanding the "why" of rapid ejaculation will not solve the problem. **The focus of this book will be on the "what" and the "how."** What is happening and how can we change it. We will take a look at some of the reasons proposed, but not be satisfied with any single theory of "why."

CIRCUMCISION

In the past, the issue of sensitivity has been actively debated between those who would trim and those who would not. There have been two diametrically opposed positions. One camp claimed that an uncircumcised man has the advantage in stay power, as nature had intended the foreskin as protection for the sensitive head (*glans*) of the penis and, when in place around the non-erect glans, this sheath of skin desensitizes the *coronal rim* (or *ridge*) by this constant contact. By this reasoning, the uncircumcised man should last longer. On the other hand, the circumcised penis, this argument continues, is more sensitive because the head is uncovered and the nerve-rich rim is exposed. Thus the expectation that a circumcised male would come quicker.

The other camp, just as convinced of their opposite view, argued that the head of a circumcised penis is indeed unprotected, but as a result gets more direct contact through it's contact with underwear. It is argued that the exposed head has therefore been somewhat numbed, and is thus less sensitive than a glans that is constantly protected by a foreskin. Thus the expectation that an uncircumcised male would be the more rapid.

The reality is that those who would argue the pros and cons of circumcision must do so on other grounds, as there is no evidence whatsoever that the presence or absence of a foreskin makes any difference in the owner's ejaculatory control. The head of a penis and, in particular the coronal rim, is very sensitive regardless of whether it is snuggled inside a pair of jockey shorts or hanging within a pair of boxers, and regardless of whether or not it is covered by a foreskin. With most uncircumcised penises, once arousal has occurred and an erection obtained, the foreskin has slid down over the head and the coronal rim is as available for stimulation as is the rim of the trimmed version. The search for a reason for rapid ejaculation must turn elsewhere, since circumcision is not the "why" in understanding nor the "how" when fixing an uncircumcised fast shooting penis.

INHERITANCE

Dan Junot, author of a small book with a big title (*Stop Premature Ejaculation and Learn to Control Male Orgasm*) notes that premature ejaculation is not inherited, but then states that there are no published research findings on the subject. He claims that in his clinical experience many rapid ejaculators "...note that their brother(s) did not have the problem." In my own clinical experience of 30 years I have never talked with a man who has compared ejaculatory speed with his siblings!

I prefer to be playful with the concept of inheritance and to go well beyond the immediate family that Mr. Junot considers. If biologically our prehistoric ancestors increased their chances of survival by ejaculating rapidly, I would argue that there is an inherited predisposition to coming quickly and it is this very assumption that allows me to think of the "problem" as something other than an "illness," a "disability," or a "disorder." Who says a man should be able to last 15 minutes when the deposit of sperm can be accomplished in 30 seconds. Other primates do it that fast, if not faster!

Remember, it is only with the evolutionary advantaged human capacity to love and the modern environmental support of our physical security that we can talk of our enjoyment of sex as a shared erotic pleasure apart from the simple act of procreation. Our ancient ancestors made babies. We can make babies also, but in addition have the technology to prevent conception and the psychology to make love.

Fast works fine in the wild and perhaps there is something to the socio/biological argument and we did inherit the quickness. This does not mean that it is useless to attempt to gain control. However, it does mean that the modern day "minute man" is neither sick nor broken... maybe he is the product of a long line of survivors.

With our capacity and desire to make grand and glorious love for the sheer fun of it, we had better figure out how to deal with some pretty old wiring! The good news is that with patience and practice, the computer can be re-programed!

ANGER

When folks think of psychology and psychiatry, they typically conjure up images of unconscious motives and dastardly drives. Mention is made of the *psychodynamics* (the devilish inner workings beneath the level of mental awareness) that directs visible behavior, these workings most often remaining disguised and undiscovered. Out of this older analytical perspective of human behavior has come two theories regarding the underlying cause of premature ejaculation. Both theories are without any experimental support whatsoever, according to professors Guy Grenier and Sandra Byers (1995) who had looked carefully at the research. As many mental health professionals still believe these old notions, they are presented here as an example of how extreme the attempts have been to assign a psychodynamic explanation to a physical behavior. You may still encounter these old ideas in books or in counseling.

The first theory somehow reasons that adult premature ejaculation has something to do with an infant's narcissistic fascination with his penis, which is assigned exaggerated importance, and with the pleasure the infant had experienced during urination! By some devious manipulations of the mind, this early infantile narcissism supposedly resulted in the adult's uncontrolled ejaculation. This theory would be laughable were it not for the thought of all those men who have paid their "shrink" to work on their narcissism in an effort to resolve their rapid ejaculation.

A nonprofessional variation on the narcissism theme is the belief held by some women that their partners really can control their coming, but are so selfish and so caught up in their own worth that they neglect to wait and go directly for their own "big O." In reality, a man who feels good about himself and good about his own pleasure will most likely take pride in giving pleasure, delaying his own orgasm until he is certain his partner is satisfied. Narcissism has nothing to do with rapid ejaculation, although we all know that men do get pretty involved in the admiration of their own sexual apparatus!

In 1974, the prominent late psychiatrist/sex therapist, Dr. Helen Singer Kaplan, proposed the theory that the unconscious culprit is really anger. She wrote of a deep-seated hatred of women. If one were to falsely assume that every woman has exquisite sensations within her vagina during intercourse, and that prolonged thrusting is really what every woman desires, the notion of symbolically denying pleasure by coming quickly makes sense (even though never proven). I have seen women who believe their partner's rapid ejaculation is a sign of hostility, but I have never spoken with a rapid ejaculator in a committed loving relationship who agrees!

This is not to deny that some men are selfish and disrespect women, and a user of women may certainly show little concern for pleasure other than his own. Not every rapid ejaculator, however, disrespects woman and not every man who disrespect women is a rapid ejaculator! Recognizing that she might have been wrong in her psychodynamic explanation, Dr. Kaplan (1989) later noted that most rapid ejaculators are without emotional or mental disorders. As intriguing as the theories might be, it is not likely that ejaculatory control (or the lack thereof) has much to do with any devious unconscious psychological demons!

AVOIDANCE OF INTIMACY

It has been observed that some men with a strong desire for sexual release, seem uncomfortable with <u>emotional</u> intimacy. Paradoxically they crave physical release but without intimate contact. Premature ejaculation, it might follow, would be a way such men could achieve physical gratification without having to establish emotional closeness. "Wham, bam, thank you ma'am!" There certainly are these men with intimacy problems and an inability to bond emotionally, but it has not been demonstrated that this is a cause of rapid ejaculation.

Although not a direct cause of the "Oops" phenomenon, a fear of intimacy certainly may be the reason some men avoid opening up emotionally and physically. It may also be why they make repeated excuses in a feeble attempt to explain why "there just has not been any time for the homework." These men complain profusely about ejaculating rapidly, but when offered a remedy, feel threatened and resist the help. It seems that such men would rather continue with their rapid ejaculations than risk emotional closeness with their partner.

Avoidance of emotional intimacy might not be the cause of rapid ejaculation, but it might certainly be the reason why some men can not commit to a "treatment" program that requires sensual and emotional closeness. Making sex and making love are quite different.... the former requires only a penis, while the latter involves the heart.

LEARNING

It was Masters and Johnson (1966, 1970) who first suggested that early conditioning and learning set men up to become rapid ejaculators. They reasoned that early sexual experiences were characterized by haste and anxiety, as the young man hurried to finish masturbation before discovery or to complete intercourse before detection. Many men will recall at least one early encounter on a living room couch, engaged in passionate juvenile exploration while simultaneously worrying about a parent entering quietly into the room. Or how many men recall an early hurried awkward adventure in the back seat of a car, weary of the local sheriff who, armed with a bright flashlight, might suddenly peer into a window?

Since the experience of hurrying is so common, books still suggest that this early learning is an important factor in the lives of rapid ejaculators. Such experiences, however, are quite common among <u>both</u> quick ejaculators and those who last longer, and there is no research evidence to support the notion that these early experiences in any way have conditioned men's ejaculatory responses. Although this is a convenient explanation, I'm waiting for scientific evidence to directly connect that adolescent apprehension with adult sexual performance.

I will suggest that it is **not what was learned** during youth, but **what was not learned!!** A young man, following his innate sexual script, is naturally going to become quickly aroused, move rapidly into exciting stimulation, and quickly reach the point of ejaculatory inevitability. Some men, early on, learned a strategy for controlling their excitement, while others did not.

EXCITABILITY

It has been proposed that rapid ejaculators become more quickly and more highly aroused than those who seem better able to control themselves, but this has not been clearly demonstrated in research studies. However, most sexologists in clinical practice would probably agree... it does seem that most premature ejaculators are quite excitable and I often tease them about rushing blindly into the altered state of consciousness I have called "**La La Land!**" In La La Land the man is so caught up in his excitement that he has no idea where he is in his rapid progression toward the point of no return. All he knows is that everything is feeling great... he's totally out of control, but doesn't even know it! All of a sudden he is there... the trigger has been pulled and, "Oh, shit," it's too late to stop!

The role of frequency must be considered in discussing excitability, as many men are more easily excited and/or more highly excited when it has been a while since their last climax.

Thus, for many men the principle "Come a lot, last forever" may seem to apply. However, there are always exceptions to the rule. There are those men who will, each and every time, make a quick short dash into La La Land, regardless of their frequency of ejaculations.

SENSITIVITY

Some clinicians have proposed that the premature ejaculator's penis must be more sensitive than that of the fellow who lasts longer. However, studies that have attempted to demonstrate this have not show a clear difference in sensitivity between those who come quickly and those who do not. If it was simply a matter of sensitivity, the desensitizing creams would work better than they do. On the other hand, we do know that many men claim that a condom will decrease the stimulation felt and dampen sensitivity. They swear they can last longer when wearing a condom.

Research, however, cautions that we can not be sure that some penises are more sensitive than anothers (although I suspect there are vast differences among men). Despite the absence of scientific support, clinical experience does suggest that there may be something about sensitivity involved in quickness to orgasm. Those who would argue against the notion that some penises are more sensitive than others would probably not debate the idea of a wide range of clitoral sensitivity among

women.   In fact, there are women who come quite rapidly...
even with the very first touch of their clitoris. We are inclined
to view ease in coming among women a distinct advantage! It
is quite a different story, however, when it is the man with the
hair trigger.

THE SABOTEUR

There have been cases where the man is sensitive and
excitable, but could establish reasonable control if it were not for
his partner. Some women, quite **unintentionally,** get caught up
in their own excitement and continue rapid and powerful
thrusts, even as the man pleads for her to stop. He then reaches
orgasm before she could experience any satisfaction and she
may then become angry with him for not having waited. Lost in
her own La La Land, she repeatedly fails to perceive her role in
her partner's rapid ejaculation.

There are also some saboteurs who might **consciously**
precipitate an early ejaculation. There are a number of reasons
for this willful sabotage. For a woman who does not enjoy the
physical act of sex, a quick ejaculation shortens the
inconvenience and possibly her physical discomfort.

For a sexually responsive woman wishing to avoid
intimacy, precipitating her partner's rapid ejaculation will
provide some brief physical pleasure but with a minimum of
emotional discomfort. It is interesting to note that some women

who are uncomfortable with intimacy pair up with a men with an identical need to avoid closeness. They become co-conspirators in the plot to shorten the sexual encounters, even though both would like a more satisfactory sexual encounter. Together they silently collude to sabotage the homework assigned in their therapy, often becoming angry with the therapist for not providing a quick fix that does not involve sensual touch and intimate contact!

If there has been a saboteur (or saboteurs) in the bed room during a couple's <u>sexual</u> rendezvous, the same sabotage is likely to be there as the couple attempts to work on ejaculatory control, even when it involves <u>nonsexual</u> tough. Be it guilt, anger, avoidance of intimacy, fear of failure, or even a fear of success, when there is resistance to the homework, something unspoken is going on. A couple's sexual concerns can not be properly addressed until all resistance is understood and any underlying personal or relationship issues are identified and resolved.

Chapter 6

NATURAL ENEMIES
OF CONTROL

SEXUAL EXCITEMENT

How can something so good, that **about-to-explode level of sexual excitement**, be so devastating in terms of a man's ejaculatory control? Let's do a review of what we have covered. Men seek sexual encounters because of a natural drive (libido). There is a powerful natural urge to merge through the insertion of an extremely sensitive part of the male anatomy into a fantastically warm and inviting part of a partner's body. This is natural... right?

The next natural thing to happen is the initiation of pelvic thrusts (which was not taught), and in the process, sliding the sensitive penis (if heterosexual) between the warm moist walls of a snug vagina. Through this thrusting motion, the shaft and sensitive head of the penis receive exquisite stimulation. It is natural and desirable to do all of this, because that is what feels good! The man feels pleasure from his thrusting and thinks how very good it feels to be in motion. The feelings emulate from deep within the pelvis... the synchronized simultaneous stimulation along the penile shaft and head are combined with this deep large muscle feedback from the hips and thighs. It is all so very natural and so very exciting!

As the good feelings grow and the arousal builds, men could ever so naturally slip into an altered state of consciousness, turning control over to our co-pilot, Mother Nature. In pursuit of nature's exclusive interest in procreation, she has sweetened the lure of the La La Land... just making it so easy to get caught up in the thrusting and the marvelous feelings of skin against skin and penis sliding within the vagina (or other warm places). When in that altered state and out of contact, the program runs on automatic... that program is simply to "get it up, get it in, get it off, and get it out!"

As a man approaches orgasm, whether he knows it or not, he is beginning to tense. This *hypertonicity* is more obvious in women and her tensing is an indication that she will probably reach orgasm if the stimulation continues. Men do not tense as much, it is generally brief, and, typically (being in motion), it is less apparent.

The man is now on automatic pilot, moving in a way that excites the sensitive nerve endings in his penis and adding internal (*proprioceptive*) feedback from his pelvis. His body tenses in the process and, he might either look at whatever parts of his partner's he can see, or close his eyes and run a mental movie in his mind. (Men, being visual creatures, typically add a variety of visual/mental images to the erotic mix.) Everything adds to the subjective experience of sublime sexual pleasure.

When highly excited, thrusting and visualizing erotic images, it is just so easy in this La La Land to lose track of the race toward the lure of that point of ejaculatory inevitability! This is particularly true if the excitement is intensified by infrequent ejaculations. Mother Nature is now in control and she wants the seed to be planted... right <u>now</u>!

SEXUAL ANXIETY

With all the sexual stereotypes and media generated expectations, and with all the meanings that get attached to sexual performance (e.g., personal value, barometer of love), it is a wonder that anyone is able to perform. In fact, as has been noted, "Sex is perfectly natural... it just isn't naturally perfect!" If we strive for perfection we will be disappointed with ourselves or our partners (or both). We will worry about our equipment and our ability to use it. The unfortunate paradox is that the more we worry about being perfect, the less likely we are to get there! And it's not just anxiety about sexual performance, general stress or other worries can also impact sexual performance.

Among clinicians it is generally accept that men with rapid ejaculation tend to be a bit more anxious in general or at least more worried about sexual abilities than are men who demonstrate better control. Unfortunately if a man with generalized anxiety is quick and begins worrying about his quickness, he might come even faster and a cycle develops. The quicker he is, the more he worries, and the more he worries the quicker he becomes. Ejaculatory control begins to fade.

If, as ejaculatory control slips away, one partner or the other becomes reluctance to initiate, fearing another unintentional quickie, they may begin actively avoiding each other. When their encounters stretch out, there is both anxiety and excitement... that potent and destructive combination that creates havoc in the bedroom.

Years ago I had seen a young college student in my office who had come in with the complaint of rapid ejaculation. I ask what is usually among my first questions... "How quickly are you ejaculating?" I thought he had misinterpreted my question when he began telling me about taking a college exam. "On the day of a test, I wake up feeling anxious. When I am sitting in the classroom waiting, I can feel my anxiety build. As the professor begins telling the class about the exam, my hands begin to perspire and I become nervous as hell. As he passes out the exam papers, placing them face down on each of our desks, it feels as though my heart is about to break out of my chest. Then as he stands again at the front of the class and says 'OK, you can now turn your papers over and begin,' I turn my exam paper over and COME!" Now that's got to be the fastest gun in the West!

I think the triggering of this student's ejaculatory reflex by skyrocketing test anxiety dramatizes the point that anxiety is a contributing factor. Since anxiety is a sort of mobilizing energy in response to some internal or external sense of danger, it might be that nature has built us to get off quicker when the danger is the greatest. As anxiety mounts Mother Nature might just be leaning close to whisper in our ear, " Get the job done <u>now</u> so you can protect your butt!" Remember, *anxiety* may sound the alarm and heighten our readiness to react, but, as we will see, *panic* has a much more destructive potential.

Chapter 7

THE HIGH PRICE OF PERFORMANCE ANXIETY

THE FEAR OF FAILURE

It is well established that stress, worry and anxiety contribute negatively to the difficulty with ejaculatory control. In addition to the deterioration of any semblance of control, when a man is "uptight," his partner will usually perceive it. If she then begins to worrying about his worrying, she is likely to have trouble with her own relaxation, arousal or orgasm. Anxiety in the bedroom is contagious and is a major cause of couples avoiding stressful sexual encounters. After all, sex is supposed to be relaxing and fun - not stressful and disappointing.

A man who rigidly believes that prolonged intercourse is the hallmark of erotic success, is likely to begin worrying obsessively about his uncontrollable orgasms. The real or imagined pressure to perform both long and well is even more intense if his partner seems also to be looking for exemplary sexual performance. As a result of all this inner turmoil (and partner pressure), tremendous *performance anxiety* is likely to be generated. It is as if his bedroom performance is being closely observed and, upon completion, a score will be given him by a panel of critical judges. With this intense pressure to do well, the man now is focused on his fear, not on his partner's response. He becomes more aware of his anxiety than even his own pleasure. Rather than being relaxed and focused on the sensual feelings he and his partner should be experiencing, he becomes tense as he critically focuses on his own performance.

In the midst of this intense apprehension, the man might suddenly realize that his anxiety has interfered with becoming erect. Now the problem is not one of ending too soon, but rather one of not being able to even begin! What began as a concern over rapid ejaculation has become a more general and very powerful *fear of failure*. This intense fear is one of the major causes of erectile disorders (*impotence*) in young healthy men. The more stress, anxiety and apprehension present, the less likely it is that a man will achieve a good erection!

The cycle is clear and is seen frequently in the sex therapist's office. A man reports that he had experienced a series of quick ejaculations. Embarrassment was felt, and possibly, disappointment was expressed by his partner. The man reports how he began to worry about control, but his anxiety only contributed to his rapid ejaculation. He worried even more and the pressure to perform was intensified. To his dismay, as his anxiety increased the firmness of his erections deceased. When the man became aware of the failure to quickly firm up, he panicked! Worse yet, he might even have ejaculate through his soft penis!

As a result of the mutual frustration, he felt that he was in very serious trouble and he (and/or his partner) might have then begun to avoid the sexual encounters, stretching them out over time. When the couple would finally get together, a considerable amount of time had passed and he felt a lot of pressure to do it right. It had been a while since they had been together, so he really wanted to do his best. He watched himself closely to see how he was doing. Masters and Johnson called this intense self monitoring behavior *"spectatoring."* The man had become a spectator at his own performance. As his fear of failure soars, he finds himself in a "damned if you do, damned if you don't" predicament. If he can't get an erection he has failed, but if he does get one he is likely to ejaculate rapidly... and that's also a failure! It's a no win situation!

There is a very interesting paradox about male sexual response and it is an important lesson to be learned when there are both erection problems and uncontrolled ejaculations. In order to *achieve* an erections a man must be able to keep from thinking about his penis and how it is doing. He dare not monitor his penis at this point, concentrating on the good feelings, but without focusing on his hardness. There is a difference between letting good feelings come <u>up</u> into awareness and mentally going <u>down</u> to check the response. **In getting an erection the man should not monitor... but once it is obtained, he's got to! That's the paradox!!**

If there are problems with getting and/or maintaining an erection, and if this is because of high performance anxiety, the erectile concerns must be addressed before beginning work on the premature ejaculation. You can't work on how you finish if you are having trouble getting started!

Chapter 8

COUPLES' HOMEWORK ASSIGNMENTS

FIRST A SHORT STORY

Before beginning to lay out some helpful homework, let me tell you a story I have told many times. I call it the story of the eager young fireman.

> On his 11th birthday Billy's father, a fireman, gave him a bright red fire truck. Billy loved the feel of it as he pushed it across the floor and was excited by the fantasy of racing to a fire and quickly extinguishing the flames. He dreamt of someday being a real fireman, just like his dad. He waited impatiently for high school graduation and hurriedly made application for admission to the city's firefighter's academy. His lifelong dream was answered when he was accepted into the training.

Bill was enthusiastic about the practice drills and continued to be quite excited by the thought of rushing to a fire and hurriedly putting it out. Learning was good, practice was fine, and fantasy was exciting, but Bill was eager to get to the real thing. He yearned for the feeling of the heat he knew to be possible only with the actual experience.

Bill graduated from the academy with high honors. On his very first day in the station a call came in and he was on the truck racing to the blaze. As he got close to the fire he could feel the heat. The sights, the sounds and the smells were incredibly exciting and before he even thought about it, his ladder was up.

Bill, hose in hand, raced to the foot of the extended ladder and climbed toward the top. Suddenly he was falling! "Oh shit!" he muttered, "I've gone over the top!" He was embarrassed that he had not anticipated the last rung of the ladder and that he had fallen before extinguishing the flames that had excited him so. He promised that he would do better the next time.

It was not long before he was again called upon to perform the task that he had so yearned for since his youth. Again he raced up the ladder and again he failed to anticipate the final rung. Once more he was muttering an "Oh shit!" as he flew over the top and plummeted down the other side. Bill began to feel even more embarrassed, as it seemed that the harder he tried, the more nervous he grew - and the worse his control became.

Repeatedly he would race up the ladder and invariably he would fly over the top before realizing he was even close. It didn't help seeing the other guys performing well and hearing the praise heaped upon them for having stayed so well and for successfully having extinguished the flames. "Certainly," Bill thought, "I am as motivated as they are, if not more so." "Surely," he reasoned, "this control should come naturally to the son of a fireman." He knew he had the same passions as his father, but could never remember his dad saying anything about falling prematurely over the top.

One day Bill saw a beauty of a fire. He felt the heat more intensely than ever before. He knew there were spectators and he knew he was expected to perform well. It was obvious that his performance would be compared with that of the other fireman, and he really wanted to do his best.

The ladder was up and extended to its full length. Bill jumped to the task. Gritting his teeth tightly and clinging firmly to his hose, he raced for the top. A moan of disappointment arose from the spectators as Bill flew wildly over the top of the ladder. Flying through the air on his way down he could be heard to exclaim, "Oh shit, I've done it again!"

Bill was sitting on the curb, head in his hands, when a veteran fireman approached him, "What's wrong young man?" the older man asked Bill, who was now looking very dejected. "I love the excitement of being a fireman, " Bill responded, "but I never can stay on the ladder long enough to get the job finished. I can get my hose up quickly, but before it can put out the fire I go over the top."

The older man was silent, recalling his own early embarrassments when he too was new at putting out fires. It was Bill who broke the silence. Obviously still wanting to look good, Bill stated, "I don't know what I am doing wrong. I am excited about squelching the flames and so I run up the ladder as quickly as I can. But I keep falling over the last rung."

After considering Bill's dilemma, the more experienced man observed, "It would seem to me that in your excitement you forget to watch where you are going, and by the time you reach the top rung it is too late to stop! The next time you head up that ladder, slow down, look ahead, and keep track of where you are. When you see that you are approaching the point of no return, stop before you get there!"

[Birch, 1996, *A Sex Therapist's Manual*]

GETTING STARTED

SENSUAL CARESS & RELAXATION

SENSATE FOCUS - STEP ONE

It was Masters and Johnson who first brought the idea of "sensate focus" into the mental health professional's bag of therapeutic tricks. Specifically, these pioneer sex researchers and therapists introduced sensate focus as a valuable tool in treating a variety of male and female sexual dysfunctions. For our purposes we will talk of *sensate focus* as the creation of a situation within which a couple can learn to *focus on sensations*. Others have used the term "non-demand pleasuring." I like to talk of it as "intimate sensual caress."

This "homework" is not complicated and the premature ejaculator and his partner need not do the entire program as outlined by Masters and Johnson. As a first step we will look at the value in focusing on sensations while engaged in non-demand non-sexual pleasuring. It provides an excellent opportunity to study your own sensations and learn about those of your partner. How? Easy!!

You and your partner must first agree to put intercourse off limits and to avoid touching each others breasts or genitals. Yes, you read correctly. **Call a moratorium on intercourse and no playing with erogenous parts!** Why? Simple!! If there has been a problem with getting too excited and too tense, and if the goal and fear has centered on having "successful" intercourse, the way to first eliminate performance anxiety is to begin working on the relaxation by changing the goal. In this non-demand atmosphere, with intercourse off limits, you can leisurely practice giving and receiving non-sexual pleasure. In the process of decreasing performance pressures many men with unreliable erections find a more consistent response when they are not feeling the demand to get it up!

For some, this will be a brand new experience, having in the past touched only as foreplay. If *foreplay* is touch that precedes intercourse, this touch is ***for play***. The goal is not prolonged intercourse... the goal is to discover the process of relaxation and the sensual exchange of mutual pleasure.

Plan to set aside an hour... with busy schedules you may need to write a reminder onto your calendar. If you are protesting that this does not allow for spontaneous encounters, let me suggest that you think of it as "scheduling your spontaneity." Many couples in having to schedule their "dates" find ways to make time available they had not realized they had. Also, you can and should always be spontaneous with your non-sexual touch between your scheduled "dates."

Remind yourself of all the previous less frequent encounters that were truly spontaneous... they were sparse, started hot, but ended quickly! Quickies can be fun when mutually agreed upon, but you would not be reading this book if you wanted spontaneous quickies all the time!

So, schedule <u>one-hour blocks</u> of time at least <u>twice in each week</u>... three times would be better, but I am realistic about busy schedules, demands of work or school, and, if they are around, the interference of kids. Once a week is perhaps too infrequent, but may be practical in terms of your schedules.

If you really can not get together more than once a week, perform the solo exercises described later to fill in the gaps. The goal of the solo self-stimulation is not to come as many times as possible during a week, but rather to find a frequency that feels very natural for you. Coming less than that frequency will mean you will have a tougher time relaxing and staying under control with your partner.

Schedule your hour at a time which is well **before** your usual bed time. When it is time to sleep, if tired, you will most likely want to hurry through your homework. Within each hour that you have scheduled, take quick showers to feel fresh, light some candles and put on some nice music (preferably something you will not sing along with). Have some warm massage oil at the bedside (or handy on the floor if this is where you prefer to be).

Lie together naked and just cuddle. Lie quietly, breath deeply and try to relax. Avoid passionate kissing and remember, breasts and genitals are off limits. **The goal is to relax, not to arouse**. Once you feel relaxed, take turns giving and receiving a soft sensual massage... erotic, but not sexual. As you are caressing your partner, think of the texture of her skin and the warmth of her body. Focus on this <u>process</u> of receiving pleasure through giving it... try to stay relaxed, as **learning to relax is one of the most important things that you must learn.** Do not rub your penis against your partner or on the bed... stay relaxed.

Do not worry about performance. Do not worry about lasting. For now, with sexual touch off limits, all you need to focus on is the joy of sensual caress... both the giving and the receiving.

Caress your partner's back, her buns and the back of her legs. When she turns over, do her shoulders and arms, tummy and legs, but avoid her breasts and genitals. If in the process of caressing your partner you feel that you are about to ejaculate, stop, get up and walk around the room... come back once you feel under control. Do the same as your partner is caressing you. Study your sensations and watch for those bodily signals that tell you were you are in terms of your relaxation and in terms of your excitement. Find that balance where you can relax, feel pleasure in giving and receiving, and, at the same time, remain in control.

Each night of your homework, trade off who gets to receive first. Both as giver and as receiver focus on relaxation and on the pleasure of giving pleasure. Talk of what feels good and learn from each other how each likes to be touched. Discover new erogenous zones, such as the feet and the smooth hollows behind the knees and inside elbows where the nerve endings reside close to the surface of the skin. Really tune in on your feelings, both as giver and as receiver, and stay playful.

I believe most couples do not touch enough, do not talk enough, and fall into a pattern where touching is only exchanged as the silent somber prelude to sex. I would love, therefore, to recommend that you spend at least two weeks with the playful non-sexual sensate focus... longer if you could only get together once during each week.

Try your best to do the sensate focus non-sexual caress for at least two weeks, at least twice per week. **Do not progress to the next step if there is anxiety or tension... you will only set yourself up for more disappointment!** Be sure that you and your partner are both relaxed and that you and she will both be comfortable with including genitals in the homework.

If you and your partner are a couple that has been avoiding each other, you may not be ready to jump right into the more sexual homework. Stay with this non-sexual step until both of you are absolutely ready to move on. Rush nothing in the process... you've got a lifetime to master this, and it might take some time to become comfortable with each other again. If, because of emotional distance in your relationship, you need the non-sexual time to grow close again and before both are ready to begin the couples sexual homework, stay with this first step. In the meantime, you should do the solo practice described later in this book.

Although this sensate focus is not intended to directly effect your rapid ejaculation, learning to relax is an essential element and in sexual encounters it is important that you know when you are tense and when you are not. In doing the non-sexual touch it is OK if you feel sexually excited. When relaxed, the exchange of this sensual touch is likely to trigger some response. The important thing is to stay in touch with the level of your arousal and, if it begins to escalate, to back off from what you are doing. If you've gone into La La Land, separate for a brief cooling off period. Talk a bit or get up and walk around.

Return to the sensual touch once you feel you are back under control.

I do worry about suggesting 14 days or more without sexual release, although you will find that <u>filling any gaps with masturbation might be essential</u> to on-going management. If you wish, once or twice a week, separate from this homework, you can have intercourse or bring each other to orgasm in other ways... but you must feel relaxed before beginning. At this stage, since you are not working directly on the control, **agree not to worry about duration**. Pleasure each other and just let the orgasms happen... being sure your partner gets her turn to come also.

Do not take advantage of the invitation to pursue an orgasmic release and neglect your sensate focus exercises. Let an orgasm be the reward for being good students and for faithfully doing your sensual homework. Do not decide midstream that a non-sexual date should be an opportunity for a quickie! Either do the agreed upon sensual homework, or agree <u>in advance</u> that it will be OK to have a quickie.

Discovering the pleasures of taking (or making) time to give and receive sensual massage allows you to return to it at any time in the future. Be sure to "stay in touch" as you move on to the more sexual assignments. **In a long term relationship, making intimate and sensual love is far more important than making genital and sexual intercourse. Learn now the pleasures of erotic caress. . . skill to be valued for a lifetime!**

SENSATE FOCUS - STEP TWO

It is important to feel relaxed and to feel some semblance of control before moving on to the second step. This step is the transition between working on relaxation and beginning the work on gaining better management of your automatic flight into La La Land. Continue to schedule your sessions - one of my client couples called these their "lube jobs," given the amount of massage oil they were lovingly and lavishly smearing on each other's body.

Now I would like the two of you to really focus in on the verbal feedback... **communication is so important in connecting intimately (and effectively) with another human being**. By now, if you are relaxed, you should be feeling enough control that you can "specialize" in giving sensual pleasure to your partner. Take time now to more fully explore her body... every nook and cranny. Be generous in your giving, as soon she will be asked to give a lot of attention to you. Yes, her breasts and genitals are now on limits! With her help, become an expert on her total body... let her words and sounds guide you. Explore your partner's body with your hands and with your mouth. Tell her how good she feels and tastes to you. Remember, "sensual" means "of the senses," not just the sense of touch. Focus on an awareness of all your senses and the pleasures they bring to your consciousness. As your hands feel your partner's contour, visually enjoy her body while listening to her soft sounds, tasting her skin and smelling her aroma. **Get in touch with all your senses!**

As you go through the homework that is coming up, always begin (or end) with a full body caress and erotic sex play for your partner. I do suggest that you give to her first, as many men lose motivation after they come. Noting this, Dr. David Schnarch, noted sex therapist, observed that women have orgasms, but men have "snorgasms!" Many women have already learned that if they want their special time, they had better get it before the guy comes... because when he finishes, it's nap time!

It is important that your partner feels that you have an interest in giving her pleasure. She will be asked to give a lot in future exercises and it is important that she knows there will be something special in it for her. Now that her genitals are on limits, do not rush... a dive for the crotch is a turn off for most women! Move slowly from a sensual massage to a sexual caress.

Remember, most women when comfortable and relaxed respond to direct clitoral stimulation. Ease up to this most sensitive "pleasure bud." Be careful if she has not already begun to lubricate, as this area is very sensitive and rubbing a dry clitoris may prove more irritating than arousing. If an artificial lubricant is needed for the sensual caress of this delicate tissue, use a safe water-soluble product such as **K-Y Jelly** or **Astroglide** and be gentle until her arousal builds.

If you have been using a massage lotion with a vegetable oil base, do not use that oil on your partner's genitals! As one can never be sure what is growing in massage oil, avoid the risk of causing a bladder or vaginal infection and keep these oils away from her genital area. Additionally, you should never use

Vaseline on a woman's genitals nor as a lubricant for intercourse, as this petroleum base jelly will not mix with a woman's natural lubrication (her *transudate*) and may actually retard her production by clogging the pores from which her wetness seeps.

Stay relaxed and do not lose track of where you are... she will understand now if you have to stop or if you get up and move. However, always remember, if you become so excited that you come when she does, do not beat yourself up and do not apologize!! This may indicate that you will need to increase the frequency of your sessions together or, in filling in the gaps, you might need to masturbate a bit more often.

Step two is essentially an opportunity to learn more about your partner and to perfect your skill in arousing and satisfying her. You may stimulate her orally if this is something you both enjoy. Do not rush this *cunnilingus*... ease into it... tease for a while... she'll appreciate the build up.

After you have pleasured your partner, following her direction and fulfilling her desires, it will be your turn. You will be starting the start/stop program at this point, assuming that you are relaxed and feeling some sense of control. The start/stop program will be described a bit later in this chapter.

Remember, if you happened to ejaculate while manually or orally caressing your partner, do not become upset and offer no apology. Rather, tell you partner of your great excitement in giving her pleasure and the enjoyment you felt as you came while caressing her.

THAT TINGLY ABOUT-TO-EXPLODE SENSATION

Before going any further, I've got to mention something important! If you have ever experienced this tingly about-to-explode sensation, you will know exactly what I'm talking about. It's an unmistakable right-on-the-edge from the very get-go sort of feeling... like don't even breath on it!! It is that feeling that the lightest touch will instantaneously trigger an explosive orgasm! The penis feels electric... the man is ready to pop and he knows it! With some men this happens only during the earliest and most exciting encounters with a new partner (novelty is a powerful aphrodisiac), but with other guys it happens on a more frequent and persistent basis. Anxiety and excitement have combined and the result feels irreversibly explosive!

There are two things you can do if this happens to you. You can just let'er rip or you can get up, start moving, and keep walking until that feeling begins to diminish. It will fade if you give it a few minutes. Then when some semblance of control returns, explain as best you can, get yourself settled down and go back to your play.

THE CLASSIC SQUEEZE TECHNIQUE

MASTERS AND JOHNSON

One can not write of the classic squeeze technique without crediting Masters and Johnson (1970) with making this approach popular. Beginning with an approach first introduced by Dr. James Semans, Masters and Johnson added their own elaboration and detail, presenting it to the public in their widely read book entitled *Human Sexual Inadequacy.* While I strongly believe that the homework assignments given a couple need not involve the squeeze, I will present it here because of its place in the history of sex therapy, because the reader will still find it written about in other self-help books, and because many clinicians still recommend it in the treatment of premature ejaculation. However, there is no research that demonstrates that the squeeze technique is any more effective than those approaches where the squeeze is not employed. We will look at it for the reasons given, but also to find clues to what might actually work.

M & J's CLASSIC POSITION

Masters and Johnson were quite detailed in the directions they gave their patients, and were very exact in what they expected. In advising a couple on the proper position for using the squeeze technique, M & J instructed the woman to sit against the headboard of her bed, propping herself up comfortably with some pillows. She was instructed to spread her legs so that her partner, resting on his back, could scoot his pelvis up to her between her open legs. With him lying in the opposite direction, she now has direct access to his genitals, as is evident in the illustration present here.

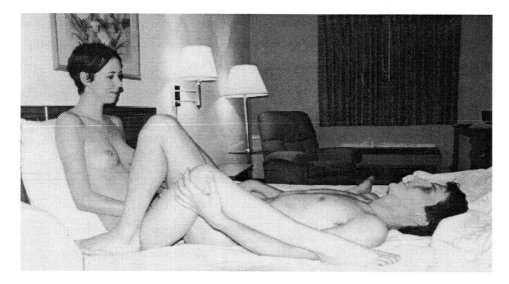

As you can see, this is a good position for stimulation of a man's penis and allows the receiver to lie back and relax. He can steal no kisses, can not reach the giver's breasts and can do little other than lie there like a good student and focus on his sensations. In the early stages of homework, I strongly recommend that the man on his back stay perfectly relaxed and keep his eyes closed! The view of his naked partner fondling his penis would distract from his responsibility to stay focused on his level of arousal. **Remember this position for use in early exercises, even if the squeeze is not being applied!**

THE ACTUAL SQUEEZE

Masters and Johnson directed the woman to place her thumb on the *frenulum*, that sensitive area on the underside of the penis where the coronal rim of the head comes around. Many men recognize this as a very sensitive area and, quite likely, one of the spots that provides the exquisite sensations responsible for high levels of excitement. While sensitive to a light touch, the pressure exerted on this spot by the partner doing the squeeze will cause no pain.

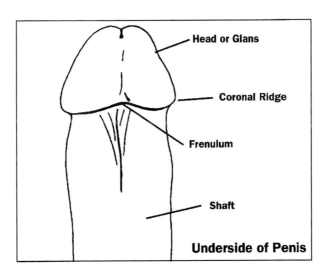

One finger is placed above the rim (or ridge) of the head and one immediately below, with the penis now being held between the thumb (on the frenulum) and the opposing fingers above and below the rim. The drawings presented here will help conceptualize this squeeze.

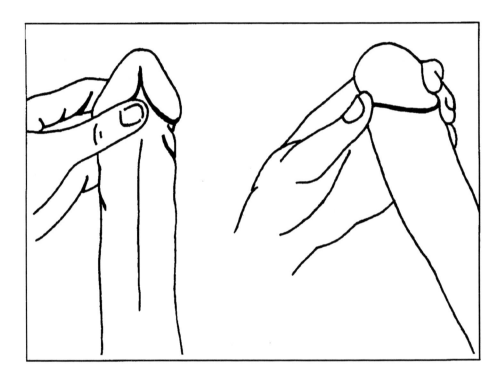

Now that we have covered the basic position and the actual squeeze, let us move on to the behavioral home work that is assigned when using this classic technique.

THE SQUEEZE TECHNIQUE - STEP ONE

With her partner's pelvis between her legs and his genitals immediately in front of her, the woman begins stroking his penis with a dry hand. The man is to lie quietly and experience the sensations as his excitement builds. As he senses his approach toward the point of ejaculatory inevitability, he signals his partner. She stops the sexual stimulation and applies pressure using the squeeze described above... thumb pressing on the frenulum. After squeezing firmly with her thumb and first two fingers for 3 to 4 seconds, she releases her partner's penis. Masters and Johnson then instruct that the woman "...should allow an interval of 15 to 30 seconds after releasing the applied pressure... and then return to active penile stimulation." These pioneer sex therapists always gave detailed and precise instructions... 3 to 4 seconds there, 15 to 30 here... no more, no less.

Over the years it has become apparent that any value to these exercises comes from the enhancement of the couple's communication and the man's ability to track his excitement. Thus, if the squeeze technique is attempted, the woman should squeeze when the man says "squeeze," hold it until the man says "I'm OK" and resume the sexual stimulation only after he says "It's safe now!"

The sequence of arousing and then squeezing is to be repeated four or five times in each session before the man ejaculates. Intercourse at this stage is forbidden by Masters and Johnson.

THE SQUEEZE TECHNIQUE - STEP TWO

Masters and Johnson have written in very clinical, medical and precise terms, often seeming somewhat mechanical in their approach. A more sensual step has been added to their basic instructions... a step in which the woman uses a lubricant on her partner's penis or, if she is comfortable, stimulates him orally. However, the sequence is the same. Four or five times in each session she is to arouse him as he monitors his excitement and, again when he signals, she squeezes the head of his penis in the prescribed manner.

Given how difficult it is to learn ejaculatory control, it is surprising to read the unrealistic statement by Masters and Johnson that "Usually two to three days of marital-unit cooperation are necessary to establish full ejaculatory control with the squeeze technique under manipulative conditions." Back in the late '60s and early '70s, these sex therapists were breaking new ground and did not want to take the risk of suggesting that unmarried couples could use their techniques. Hence they always refer to husband and wife or, as in this quote, "the marital unit." Also, think "playful sensual fondling" as the translation of what in their sterilized clinical language they have called "manipulative conditions."

Two to three days to gain enough control to move on??? I think not! But let's look at their next step.

THE SQUEEZE TECHNIQUE - STEP THREE

In their stiff clinical jargon, Masters and Johnson have written "Establishing security of response relative to the squeeze technique is but the first step in a therapeutic progression that moves from onset of successful ejaculatory control under manipulative influence to a controlled coital process." Translation. . . after having practiced the phase involving the woman's erotic play with her partner's penis, it's time to get him inside! We'd say, "put it in and sit still," but our pioneers referred to this as "non-demanding intromission."

Specifically, the man lies flat on his back and relaxes. After stimulating him manually and employing the squeeze as needed two or three times, his partner straddles him and guides his penis into her vagina. To quote M & J, "Once mounted, she should concentrate on retaining the penis intravaginally in a motionless manner, providing no further stimulation of her husband by thrusting pelvically." Some variations of this step would even have the woman stuff a partial erection into her vagina as she hovers over him.

While I would never recommend the stuffing procedure (seems kind of silly to me) I will be saying a lot more about the female superior position with the man lying passively on his back. **Remember the formula: Woman on top + passive man below = greater opportunity to monitor excitement!**

The reasoning behind the non-demanding intromission is that it will allow the man, in a non-threatening passive position, to experience the feeling of vaginal containment. Even without movement, some men will continue their progression toward ejaculatory inevitability. If this happens he should signal his partner who then dismounts, grabs his penis and squeezes as directed. Once he is back under control, she re-mounts.

THE SQUEEZE TECHNIQUE - STEP FOUR

Although not detailed by Masters and Johnson, most advocates of the squeeze technique would move quickly now to a step during which the woman provides manual or oral stimulation a couple times, squeezing as required, before mounting her partner as above. Now, however, she would be instructed to move up and down on her passive partner's penis. By now you know... he is to keep close track and, as he feels himself approaching that point of no return, he signals his gal. She jumps off, grabs his penis and applies the traditional squeeze. The procedure is repeated four or five times before he eventually comes.

THE SQUEEZE TECHNIQUE - STEP FIVE

Now intercourse can be a bit more active, with the partner still on top but now with some thrusting also by the man. Four or five times with disengagement and squeezing. Some therapists might suggest that she simply needs to raise up, but not completely off of her partner. She can, having elevated herself, squeeze at the base of his penis... thumb against the softer under side. Still others have advised that she could just stay in close, lean back and gently pull on her partner's scrotum! This latter somewhat eccentric maneuver seems to be based on the assumption that preventing the testicles from pulling up will decrease the urge to ejaculate. Anything but a gentle tug would certainly decrease most all of his urges!

With this fifth step accomplished (with or without its variations), the invitation is to try other positions and the assumption seems to be that by now, control should have been achieve.

OBSERVATIONS

I will first of all remind you that I do not belief in a quick or permanent "cure." Any effective homework must teach a man a strategy that he might need to follow for a life time. I can't just give you a fish... I've got to teach you how to fish on your own!

Earlier in the book I had stated that VCRs come with detailed complicate manuals, and penises don't. Well, some of the self-help books on "curing" premature ejaculation make technical instructions for an electronic device seem like first grade reading.

Some sex manuals talk of "desensitizing the frenulum." This surprises me when stated by an intelligent professional, as there is no other skin surface that can be desensitized simply by applying pressure for a few seconds a couple times a week! I find no evidence for the desensitization notion... it does not make neurological sense!

I have seen many couples who, in their quest for an easy cure, have labored through the long difficult medical books by Masters and Johnson, or who have read less clinical self-help books on the topic. There have been those who flat-out could not understand the procedure and did not even attempt it. M & J wrote their first books for the professional community, expecting to sell a few to physicians and psychologists. In a time when our society was hungry for accurate sexual information and in desperate search for solutions to sexual concerns, the general public consumed these early works with great gusto. Sales soared beyond the writers' wildest dreams. Unfortunately, for many the original books were too dry and quite difficult to understand.

Many who did manage to work their way through the clinical language and medical minutia or who found easier texts to read were confused by the instructions... uncertain exactly where the thumb was to be place, how hard to squeeze there, and how long to hold it. It did not help that the books seemed to imply a quick remedy. Many couples gave it a try, only to find that it was not helping, with women feeling guilty that perhaps they were not squeezing the right spot!

Some couples read about the squeeze and actually thought it was supposed to hurt! At that point either the woman said to her partner, "I can't do that to you," or he said to her, "No way am I going to let you squeeze my dick!"

Finally I have seen those couple that tried, following the directions as closely as possible, but misinterpreted when the squeeze was to take place. The tip off is when the guy says, "She squeezed the head of my penis, but I came anyway!" It is obvious that he was not signaling her until he had actually reached the point of ejaculatory inevitability... and by then it was too late!! He was not monitoring the subtle increase in pleasure and was only yelling when the obvious brink of disaster had already been reached! **Remember, regardless of your homework, one of the keys is to learn how to stay in touch with your level of arousal even when it is low, to feel it built, and to do something to stop or delay the escalation while you still have some control!**

THE POPULAR START-STOP METHOD

START/STOP - STEP ONE

Let's take a moment to reflect on the classic squeeze. The partner stimulates her passive mate as he lies there tracking his arousal. As he feels that he might be approaching the point of ejaculatory inevitability, he signals or tells her to stop... at which point she stops the exciting stimulation and squeezes. If she is not actually desensitizing his frenulum, why bother with the squeeze?

Essentially the start/stop procedure is very similar to the squeeze program, but without the squeeze! It makes sense! If the man's responsibility is to learn how to track his arousal and to stop or delay ejaculation by stopping or changing the stimulation, the squeeze becomes immaterial!

This is how I would structure the first step of your homework, perhaps better described as "homeplay." Plan a realistic number of sessions per week, giving them the time and priority that you had with the sensate focus exercises. In each episode, be sure to pleasure your partner so that she will not feel neglected. Remember, for <u>her this is step two of the sensual caress assignment</u>. When it is your turn to receive, lie down and begin to relax.

Your partner can assume M & J's classic position propped against the headboard, or she can sit beside you... whatever is most comfortable for her. It should be her preference. She should begin with some non-demand touch, caressing your body in non-sexual ways as you continue to relax. At this point you can be focusing in on the feeling of your partner's hands on your body and of any sexual response to this.

Once you feel relaxed, in control and aware of your body's signals, your partner can begin caressing your penis. Imagine that you are at the foot of a ladder. Keep close track and, as your excitement grows, imagine that you are beginning to climb up that ladder, a rung at a time. It is your job to keep yourself from falling over the top, so you must look ahead in order to anticipate that point of no return. As your partner moves from non-sexual touch to the stroking of your penis with her dry hand, you will experience yourself beginning to climb more quickly. Now your focus must shift from the sensation of her hand stroking your penis to where you are on that ladder. **To focus only on the erotic sensation is to stand dangerously close to the gates of La La Land, that altered state of consciousness where Mother Nature eagerly awaits you!**

Lie perfectly still! Do not move and do not tense. Keep you eyes closed and avoid any sexual thoughts or images... you need to be concentrating on where you are on that ladder. When you feel close to the point of no return, tell your partner to stop. At this point she should let go and sit back, and you will feel yourself level off and begin descending that ladder. Do not worry about M & J's 15 to 20 seconds... do not ask your partner to start again until you are absolutely sure that you are back under control and standing at the foot of that ladder. Once settled and back under control, signal that she can start the stimulation again.

At this step sexual stimulation should be minimized. **No oral stimulation of your penis is allowed and your partner's hand must be dry. Even then, she should stroke slowly.** You will not add any muscle feedback if you stay relaxed and there will be no hypertonicity. With eyes closed and mind devoid of erotica, mental contribution is minimized. This gives you the necessary time to experience those inner indicators of arousal and to begin learning how to effectively monitor your level of arousal. Start and stop 5 or 6 times before allowing yourself to ejaculate and when you do, see if you can identify what it was you did to give yourself permission to come. It is good to learn how not to ejaculate, but also to know how you let go so you can.

I recommend that you stay at this stage for no less than two weeks, but I always feel that staying longer at each step allows for better learning. Longer at each level is absolutely necessary for the guys who come each time with the slightest touch. Do not rush any of these steps, as it is better to learn what you need to learn the first time through. This homework should not be too frustrating, as with each session you will have the opportunity to ejaculate with your partner's manual stimulation. Intercourse is off limits for now, but have fun exploring your partners' various erotic avenues to achieving orgasm.

If you need to increase the frequency beyond what is comfortable for your partner, fill the gaps with the solo practice described later in this book. Do not attempt to pressure your partner into a frequency greater than what she desires. It is far better to take care of the excess yourself than to risk turning off your partner.

START/STOP - STEP TWO

Continue to schedule your "dates," ideally being able to work in two or three sessions per week. I am amazed by how others have unrealistically advised couples to do their homeplay every single night! That is not practical for most couples, and pressure to get it done with the prescribed frequency risks turning an otherwise fun exercise into work. In addition, if a couple does actually force a nightly practice ritual while practicing, they will not really have prepared themselves for their more typical and more widely spaced routine.

When you have made the time that fits best into your schedules, start as before with some play for your partner. Remember, if at any time your arousal suddenly begins to escalate or you have one of those tingly about-to-explode experiences, stop everything and, if needed, get up and walk! Stay in touch with your feelings and, once settled, come back to bed.

Be sure to excite and satisfy your partner in the ways that she loves to be pleasured. Spoil her... she'll surely return the favor! When it is your turn to receive, you partner should stimulate you with her dry hand, starting and you stopping her one or two times. Then she should use a lubricant of your choice... warmed if possible. If she is comfortable with it, she can also mix in some oral stimulation for you. Regardless of the stimulation, you must keep track and stop her before reaching the last rung of that imaginary ladder. The use of a lubricant and the option of oral stimulation makes this step more exciting than the last. Be careful. Do not play brinkmanship, as you will be risking an unplanned ejaculation. Stay relaxed and do not move. Do not fantasize and, when it is time to really concentrate on your level of excitement, keep your eyes closed. Think of that ladder and stop your partner before it is too late. **Remember, it is better to stop ten strokes too soon than to stop one stroke too late!**

Within each episode, start and stop 5 or 6 times and do this homeplay step for at least two weeks (if not longer). Do not rush things!

START/STOP - STEP THREE

Continue with your scheduling, but check with each other to be sure that neither of you are feeling pressured. It is absolutely essential that your time together remains fun and relaxing. Intimacy and caring remain top priority, ejaculatory control is somewhere down the list. Between the two of you, re-affirm that! Hopefully, however, in working on the control you have both been working on more open communication and on acquiring a greater appreciation of the <u>process</u> of starting slowly with non-demand and non-sexual caress. Do not lose the desire for sensuality as we move on to the more sexual levels.

Begin each scheduled session with an exchange of non-sexual caress and, as always, find out what you can do for your partner. When it is your turn to receive, get on your back again and relax! Nothing new here! Stay calm and do not move. With eyes closed, experience your arousal as you partner caresses your penis. Start and stop two times. Now she should stroke our penis briefly with a good safe water soluble lubricant - for this good old inexpensive **K-Y Jelly** will do. After getting you good and slippery, your partner should straddle you, nestling down on you so that your penis is between the lips of her genitals (her *vulva*). With the artificial lubricant and any of her own lubrication, she should slide front to back, but without inserting your penis into her vagina.

Intercourse must remain off limits, but this "outercourse" is perhaps the next best thing. Sliding back and forth with lots of lubrication should feel good to both of you... but you must still keep track and stop her when it gets to feeling too good. Start and stop 5 or 6 times during these sessions, and repeat this step for three weeks. <u>During the first week</u> do not put your hands on your partner and keep your eyes closed. However, <u>during the second of those weeks</u>, open your eyes and put your hands on your partner's hips or thighs.

Be careful and keep track... always ready to say "Stop." Learn also how to monitor the impact of the stimulation you are getting through your eyes and your hands. Subtract this out as you near the point where you must stop, closing your eyes and removing your hands. If you feel your excitement level off, carefully ease a little closer to the point where you must stop. When you must stop her during the first and second weeks, she should lift up, breaking the contact between her vulva and your penis. Do not move. Feel yourself drop off the high level of excitement and, when you are sure you are back under control, invite her to sit and slide again.

<u>During the third week</u> I would like you to start easing more of the erotic aspects back into your awareness. Start with the visual, a bit more tactile stimulation, and then some touching of your partner's breasts. Allow a little fantasy, but do not move and stay perfectly relaxed. Feel your partner's warm slippery vulva sliding over your penis... but go back to monitoring, from

time to time checking your position on that ladder. Stop your partner's movement only after decreasing your own inner stimulation (stopping the visual input, stopping the touch, etc.). If you feel your excitement level off, ease a little closer to that point. Be careful!

At first you had her lift up when you stopped her, but during this third week I would like you to see if you can settle yourself during each pause with your partner maintaining genital contact with you. Begin adding to your directions. Initially you just had two instructions - "start" and "stop." Now add "slow down," "easy," "don't move," and "lift up." You must stop when you are nearing that dangerous point or heading recklessly into La La Land, but short of that, begin to practice changing the stimulation rather than terminating it. Feel the good feelings of that warm contact, but also keep track of your excitement level. Ease a little closer... slow her... stop her for a moment... a short

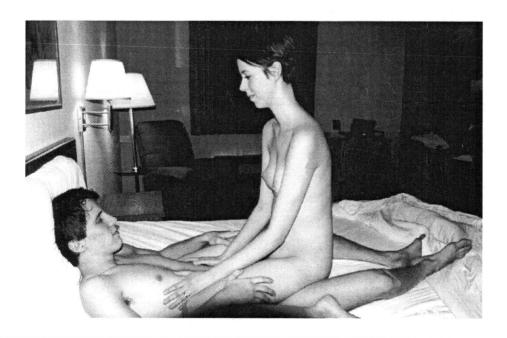

break as she sits quietly, warming your penis between the lips of her vulva. Keep track and see if you can level off at a high level of excitement and still feel some sense of control. Be careful! Keep track.

START/STOP - STEP SIX

After three weeks of the outercourse homework, each week having added something more erotic, it is time to take the plunge... literally! After the usual non-demand start and the gentle exchange of sensual caress, and after taking turns with some mutual genital play **(the start/stop variety for you)**, get on your back and relax.

Your partner should now straddle you and, for a few moments, just sit on you. Experience the warmth of her genitals against your penis, visually appreciate what you can see of her body, and rest your hands on her thighs. At the same time, with that split-screen you have hopefully developed, monitor your level of excitement. Once you feel settled, have your partner begin to slide, signaling her verbally or with your hands. Watch her body, feel the power of her pelvic movement, sense her warmth and wetness... but keep track. Getting too excited? Close your eyes, clear your mind, think of taxes! Slow her or stop her if necessary.

There are those who would discourage your thinking of baseball scores or, my favorite, imagining a pending audit by the dreaded IRS. Those who would not approve of using mental diversion believe that this distracts from the monitoring of arousal, the only task a man should focus on. While this may be true at earlier stages of the homeplay, by now I feel that a mental distraction can be quite helpful. Since it is natural for a man to conjure up erotic fantasies and explicit mental images, a "thought wedge" can disrupt this process. Wedge these non-sexual thoughts into the stream of sexual imagery... just long enough to help slow things down. By now you should be able to count backwards by 5s and monitor your arousal at the same time.

Once you are certain that you are relaxed and under control, instruct your partner to insert your erection into her vagina. It is important that there has been sufficient play to arouse your partner, as the presence of her natural lubricant is essential for an effortless penetration. Sitting astride you, she should guide your penis to her vaginal opening and slowly lower herself onto you. She should then become completely motionless, and so should you!

Feel your excitement build with this wonderful feeling of containment. Should you ejaculate with the first engulfment of your penis, do not worry and do not apologize. This might happen the first time... after all, it may have been weeks since you were "allowed" this grand entry. If it is unavoidable this first time, just let'er rip and enjoy your coming inside your partner. If this happens over several encounters, consider the possibility that you may need to increase the frequency of your joint encounters or of the masturbation that you have been using to fill any gaps. You might even want to back up in your homework, starting again at a level where you feel you had successfully gained mastery.

If you can stay under control with your partner mounted on top of you and your penis snuggled passively within her vagina, signal her to begin moving. It is important that she lean forward, supporting herself with her arms, and that she stay in tight against you. Her movements should be from front to back, not up and down. There are three reasons why I recommend sliding back and forth, rather than riding up and down. First, it is easier on your partner's legs if she does not have to bounce. Second, most women will discover (if they have not already done so) that they can get superb stimulation by staying in close and rubbing their clitoris against the base of the man's erection. Actually, as she slides forward she is sliding onto the man's pubic bone at the base of his penis, and as she slides back she is running her clitoris up the shaft of his erection.

The third reason has to do with that hard-wired program... the one that says, "You must thrust long and deep, sliding your sensitive penis full length between the walls of that moist and friendly vagina." When you are flat on your back, relaxed and completely motionless, with your partner on top doing the sliding movement, there is no proprioceptive (internal) feedback from your pelvic muscles. Equally important is that by staying in close, the stimulation provided by the muscles surrounding the opening of your partner's vagina is primarily at the base of your penis, not running along its full length. Not exactly what Mother Nature had in mind!

Keep track. Let mental stimulation in, but wedge it out if you need to settle yourself. Visually enjoy your partner's breasts as she hovers and moves over you, but close your eyes if it starts to become intense. Dare to move just a little, but keep your trusting minimal and be ready to relax if you need to calm yourself.

Within each encounter, start and stop as many times as you wish, as you are no longer under my strict homework requirements. Keep the frequency up and, after several weeks, begin experimenting with the positions I recommend... always thrusting slowly and with shorter strokes. Once you feel confident that you can read your body's signals, can monitor the level of your arousal, and can modify the stimulation so as to hover at a nice level of excitement, branch out and try some other positions... but always being very careful!

Chapter 9
GOING SOLO

PRACTICING WITHOUT A PARTNER

It is much easier to learn and maintain ejaculatory control when the man is in a stable relationship with a steady partner who is both understanding and responsive.   But what about the guy who is without a partner or whose partner is uncooperative. It is possible to work on control alone, but it is like trying to learn to play golf during the winter by watching a video and putting golf balls across the livingroom carpet into a coffee cup. While alone a man may perfect that skill, but when spring comes and, for the first time, he is out on a real course with a real friend, things are a lot different! The excitement is far greater, but so too is the pressure!

If you have no partner at all, do not avoid masturbation. As someone once said, "Masturbation is making love with your best friend." There is no pressure to perform and no critic to judge your endurance. **Find the frequency which works best for**

you. Some guys can masturbate successfully every day of the week, while the most natural frequency for others might be once within the same period of time. This is not a competition! Every day is OK and once a week is OK!! **What is important is to know your natural schedule and then maintain it.** You will know you are pushing your limits if you find that you have to work to reach orgasm. The object is not to try to see how many times per week you can come... the object is to establish your own unique pattern. You will know that you are not masturbating enough if you feel horny for a couple days and ejaculate rapidly even when you are trying to work on your control.

Most men masturbate by "jacking off," the up & down stroking of the penile shaft with a hand. The stimulation experienced is similar to the in and out stroking during intercourse, although a man will typically grip his erection tighter than the grip of a woman's vagina and the stroking is usually faster. This hard fast movement is why the practice is also referred to as "pounding your pud" and "beating your meat." At no time during the early attempts to maintain control should the stroking be hard and fast, as the solo participant at this point wants to come as close as possible to the experience of being inside a vagina. A vagina doesn't grip like a tight fist!

Men who have learned to masturbate in other ways (e.g., rubbing on their bed, using a vibrator, or stroking with an artificial vagina) should practice the first steps of the following exercises with the more traditional hand stroking. Go slow and take your time... you will not learn control overnight. An investment of time and a whole lot of patience is going to be required.

FIRST STEP IN GOING SOLO

Set aside enough time to relax and quietly think about what you want to accomplish. Nothing within these steps should be rushed. **Slow, easy and relaxed are the key words.**

Establish your own frequency of desire and, each time you masturbate, do so without a lubricant and without visual stimulation. Do not fantasize. It should be obvious that these restrictions are intended to minimize the amount of stimulation and maximize your ability to stay focused on your level of arousal. With a slow light stroke, do the Start/Stop technique described above, within each episode starting and stopping a least 5 times before allowing yourself to ejaculated. Remember, you must **monitor** your level of excitement and **stop** the stimulation <u>prior</u> to reaching the point of ejaculatory inevitability. Get in touch with those inner signals, do not lose track and do not play brinkmanship with that trigger point.

Use this time to identify what is happening within your body as your excitement builds, thinking of this like running up the steps of a ladder. After starting and stopping the desired number of times, decide that you want to come. Ease into it, experiencing fully that approach to the point of ejaculatory inevitability. Continue with the slow stroking until you orgasm. Did you experience what you did to maintain control as you anticipated that last rung of the ladder, and then what you did to let go and fly over the top. What was different when it was time to come? Did you tense somewhere in your body? Did you automatically stroke harder or faster? Was it just more of the same stimulation, but with a psychological shift from monitoring your level of arousal to experiencing the erotic pleasure? You must learn to identify what is going on before you will know how to bring yourself under control.

Repeat this first step on your own schedule for two or three weeks... or better yet, until you are absolutely sure you have learned how to keep close tabs on what is happening. It is better to take too long practicing a step than it is to hurry ahead. Slow, easy and relaxed!

If you feel that you are out of control at any point in the following steps, return to this dry hand approach and re-learn the control with less stimulation. Then after two weeks of repeating this less exciting routine, move ahead again.

SECOND STEP IN GOING SOLO

Stay relaxed! Do not attempt a practice session if you feel anxious or tense. Remember, anxiety has no place in your sex life... alone or with a partner.

Once you feel as though you have mastered the ability to predict and prevent your ejaculation with the dry hand start/stop program, add a lubricant. Some men find Vaseline works, some have used soft margarine, while others might prefer K-Y Jelly. Whatever works! With water soluble lubricants, such as K-Y, it is wise to have a container of warm water handy. A little water added to the lubricate as it begins to feel gummy will bring the slipperiness back. Whatever your lubricant is, it is good to warm it if you can... wanting to begin to approach that warm slippery feeling of vaginal intercourse.

Avoid visual stimulation and fantasy during this step. Stay relaxed and **do not move** anything but your hand. Do the lubricated start/stop on your usual schedule and again, within each episode start and stop 5 or 6 times before allowing yourself to ejaculated. Sense the difference between control and permission to "head for home." Practice this step for two or three weeks, or until you are absolutely sure that you are under control and can accurately track your inner awareness.

THIRD STEP - GOING SOLO

Are you feeling any anxiety? If so, put your sessions off until you feel relaxed. Hopefully you are getting the message... **it is important that you feel relaxed both mentally and physically.**

As you move toward feelings that are much more natural and stimulation that is much more arousing, continue as before with the lubrication, but now begin adding visual and mental images and rich sexual fantasies. Continue with the start and stop formula as before, and **continue to monitor your arousal** even as you attempt to add more and more sexual stimulation. Keep the relaxation and remember not to move anything but your hand. Stay with your personal frequency and with each encounter, start and stop at least five times before allowing yourself to ejaculate.

Are you keeping track now? Can you sense the climbing of that ladder of excitement and anticipate the point of ejaculatory inevitability well before getting to it? Practice this step for two or three weeks, or until you are absolutely sure you are ready to move on.

FOURTH STEP- GOING SOLO

Now you can become creative. If you had an alternative approach to masturbation, try it now with the start/stop principle in place. Continue with the lubrication... try some new ones. Enrich your fantasies and bring in some new visual material. Try different positions, add some pelvic thrusts, buy a vibrating toy, or purchase one of those artificial vaginas or masturbation sleeves sold in the adult toy catalogs. Above all else, as you increase your arousal with added stimulation, **keep track** of your excitement level and, as before, start and stop at least 5 times before coming.

FIFTH STEP - GOING SOLO

Continue now as in step four, but rather than stopping, **slow** your stroke and attempt to **hover** at a high state of arousal... not so high that you flirt with that flash point, but with more arousal than in previous steps. Again I will remind you that you need to **keep very close track** of your excitement and, although trying to maintain control at a higher level, be careful!

As you are approaching that point of inevitability, **slow** your stroke, **look away** from any stimulating visual material, **stop** any movement in your pelvis, **relax** any tension you feel and **end** any fantasy that you might have been having. Without stopping, minimize that stimulation... bare bones stuff as you feel yourself settle down to a safe level. Stop if you feel you ventured too close and are about to lose control.

As you feel your excitement drop with decreased input, increase the combined stimulation again... slowing and/or stopping five or six times before letting go... and even then, ease into it! Are you aware of what you did to give yourself permission to let go?

Chapter 10

A FIRST TIME STRATEGY

THAT SCARY FIRST PLUNGE

As has been said, learning ejaculatory control with a partner is a great deal easier than trying to learn alone. Obviously, not every one with these concerns is in a relationship, and, in fact, some guys might even avoid becoming involved because of their rapid ejaculation. So, what about the fellow who is currently without a sexual partner. As mentioned above, there are things he can do by himself as he practices solo in anticipation of a sexual encounter.

New relationships should not be avoided, as one can never learn ejaculatory control with a woman if women are shunned. Remember, you will never learn to play golf if you avoid going to the golf course.

If a man is looking for an emotional and sexual companion, he will at some point be put to the test. With no first time strategy for coping with new encounters, he is most likely to be quite apprehensive about those exciting/frightening first times. As we have seen, excitement and anxiety will contribute to that feared outcome... the uncontrolled rapid ejaculation.

I have talked with many premature ejaculators who delay becoming sexually involved, not wanting to deal with the predictable embarrassment of coming too soon. When the passion mounts and the clothes start coming off, anxiety sky rockets. Many a reader will have been in a similar situation and know what goes on mentally. The man starts thinking, "What if I come too fast? What will she think when it happens? What will I say to explain it? Will she ever want to see me again?" With all of these thoughts and fears racing through his head, if he has managed to get an erection, he takes the plunge. Often that no-win situation develops for the man... either he can't get an erection or he does and ejaculates almost immediately..

If the man is afraid he'll lose control, worries about his partner's disappointment, and figures he's going to have to do some serious apologizing, isn't it obvious that the man already knows he'll ejaculate quickly. However, he is not telling his partner, allowing her to formulate her own expectations... to build her own hopes of how the encounter will go. She might be looking forward to a prolonged session involving all of her favorite positions, but suddenly and unexpectedly, the man who has aroused her now moans "Oh Shit!" and comes! He knew it would happen, but she didn't! He must try to explain, apologize or beat himself up to prove to her that he really had intended to be spectacular!!

Many men wrap much of their male ego around their image as a competent sexual performer. The thought of admitting to a woman any lack of knowledge or any apprehension is unthinkable. However, I strongly believe that the best strategy for a new experience is to **forewarn** the unsuspecting woman! It is amazing to me that so many man recoil in shock when I suggest this, asking "You mean I've got to admit I have a problem???"... as if she's not going to discover it on her own!!!

I will once more suggest that thinking of rapid ejaculation as a "problem" only contributes to discomfort and loss of sexual self-esteem. I suggest a strategy such as the following. As the excitement mounts and the touching progresses, the man begins to talk. Remember, women usually love *pillow talk.* "I love how you feel... you excite me so! I want to make you feel good... to learn everything I can about your fantastic body. I want to know what feels best... what works best for you." With this reassurance he has told her of his desire to give her pleasure, and now it is time to do everything possible to give her all the non-coital pleasure she desires.

"You excite me so much!" he repeats. "I think I am so excited that I probably will not last very long. Let's not worry about me this time... this will be for you. Help me learn how to give you pleasure... I'll get my turn later." When it is time for intercourse (which should never be rushed into) he should use one of the positions recommended below, starting and stopping as best he can during these early encounters. "Wow, don't move!

You are driving me wild! Stay still for a moment... you feel so very very good!"

After his orgasm he offers **no apologies**. Rather he should congratulate her. "Wow, that was fantastic for me... didn't last long, but you really felt great to me... just could not hold back. That was wonderful... next time we'll work on lasting a bit longer... but right now I just want to hold you."

This is so much more positive than what typically happens! It reassures the woman that the rapid ejaculation was not a selfish act... remember, many women misinterpret the motives of a man who comes quickly. It opens up the communication about what feels good to the woman... remember, **each woman is unique** and men are not natural born mind readers. The strategy also introduces the idea of an ongoing relationship in which, as a couple, they can talk and work on achieving better ejaculatory control. Most important, however, is that in forewarning the woman, the man has decreased the pressure he feels to impress her with his control (he already has admitted that he has none) and the couple are more likely to share a fun playful encounter, each having positive feelings as they snuggle together in the afterglow of each other's orgasm.

Chapter 11

POSITIONS THAT HELP

BEWARE OF THE MISSIONARY POSITION

There is a story that has been told and retold many times about the naming of the "missionary position," that typical human arrangement where the woman lies on her back with legs spread and knees bent. The man lies on top between her legs, often supporting his weight on his arms. Typically in this position the man positions his body such that he accomplishes a straight shot directly into his partner's vagina. He does this by staying a bit low on her body, dropping his hips down between her open thighs.

The man, being strategically positioned for direct entry, begins pelvic thrusts with long deep strokes, achieving maximum stimulation for himself... but in most cases he is completely missing the woman's clitoris. He is too low on his partner's body and the straight shot into her vagina puts his penis well below the location of her most sensitive spot. For most women, there is not enough clitoral stimulation in this position and her freedom to move is quite limited. Although the missionary position may feel good to the woman, it feels great to the man and is more likely to bring the man to orgasm than it will her.

The story of the naming of this male superior position goes as follows:

> Many years ago a well intend band of missionaries travel to a distant land, discovering that the uninhibited natives were out in the bush joyfully going at it in every conceivable way. Both the men and the women were having fun and having orgasms. The missionaries, believing that seeking sexual pleasure was sinful, were appalled by this hedonistic behavior. Viewing such matters of the flesh as wanton and lustful, they immediately intervened, stopping the natives from their playful and creative encounters,
>
> The missionaries were faced with a serious dilemma however. On the one hand they believed that fornication was evil, but simultaneously believed that procreation was blessed. They were caught between directing these heathens to "sin not," and advising them to "go forth and multiply." A compromise had to be reached, whereupon the missionaries went out among the people, teaching that the only moral way to make a baby is with the submissive woman looking upward toward heaven and the dominant man on top.

It is impossible to know the real story of the naming of the position, but this tale makes a point. If you want to be scriptural, it would make sense to assign the male the superior role, with the woman remaining relatively passive in a subordinate position. If you were to believe that pleasure is immoral, then you would want to prescribe a position in which the woman receives no clitoral stimulation, lest she sin by feeling erotic pleasure. You would then position the man so he can thrust long and deep with powerful pelvic thrusts, bringing him rapidly to the planting of his seed. If he must feel pleasure in the performance of this procreative act, at least his sinfulness would be brief! The missionary position is not the best position for providing direct clitoral stimulation nor is it one in which the thrusting male can best maintain his control.

This traditional male superior position may feel great to both, but the woman may be unable to orgasm in this position and the man may ejaculated too quickly. The missionary position should therefore be reserved for later, once good ejaculatory control has been achieved. It is best if your early coital encounters employ positions that minimize male pelvic thrusting, decrease the penile stimulation of long deep strokes, and (as a side benefit) maximize the opportunity for stimulation of your partner's clitoris.

THE COITAL ALIGNMENT TECHNIQUE

The coital alignment technique, or CAT position, is described in detail by sexologist Ed Eichel in the 1992 book entitled *The Perfect Fit.* Basically, the strategy is to get the male and female bodies aligned in such a way that the man's penis will rub against the woman's clitoris and simultaneously the woman can rub her clitoris against her partner's erection.

To accomplish the CAT maneuver the woman should lie flat, legs apart, but not bent at the knees as she would do in the missionary position. In the missionary position she would spread wide to make room for her partner's hips, and bend her knees to raise her own pelvis. This allows for the straight shot that unfortunately misses the clitoris. The man's penis is pointing forward and the long thrusting is in the direction of the woman's head.

In the CAT position the woman's body is flat, her legs separated but straight, and her pelvis is not elevated. Her partner lies on top, sliding down to make the initial penetration, but then pulling his body up on her body so that their two pubic bones are aligned. At this point his penis is directed downward, passing over his partner's clitoris as it enters her vagina. Penetration is not deep.

I believe that the secret to the success of the CAT position, once the couple is in place, is their ability to keep their pubic bones together and to "rock," with the man going up and the woman going down, the man going down as the woman rocks up, etc. They must maintain the physical contact of their pubic bones, the rocking must be synchronized, and the man must stay high on his partner's body so that they are rubbing her clitoris against the base of his penis.

Dr. Eichel has advocated this position as an alternative in which women may learn to become reliably orgasmic with intercourse. For the woman to have an opportunity to discover if she can in fact climax in this position, the man must be able to maintain control. I believe that the elimination of the long deep thrusting and the minimal involvement of pelvic muscles provides an excellent opportunity for the rapid ejaculator to monitor his response and maintain adequate control... giving his partner time to discover her best maneuver.

It is also possible to align pubic bones and simultaneously rock with the woman on top. The man lies flat with his legs together. His partner straddles and inserts his penis, then sit quietly for a moment as he settles himself beneath her. She then lies flat on him, low on his body with her legs falling to either side of his.

He will feel his penis being brought to an almost upright position as it passes over his partner's clitoris on its way to her vagina. As in the male superior CAT, the couple rock with the woman having a bit more ability to control the movement when she is on top. The man remains relatively pasive with short slow thrusts, starting and stopping as needed.

THE FEMALE SUPERIOR POSITION

It is the female superior position that I most highly recommend as the first position of intercourse to use after completing the non-coital homeplay. As mentioned earlier, the man should lie flat and remain perfectly relaxed as his partner straddles him and guides his erection into her vagina. There should be a moment or two of quiet motionless engagement. Then the woman finds an angle that works best for her, usually one in which she is leaning forward.

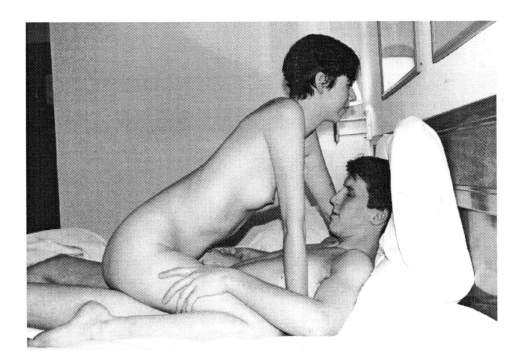

The secret to this position is the front to back sliding motion of the woman. If the man remains passive, this sliding (scooting) movement allows the woman to discover her exact pace and the perfect angle of her pelvis that will allow her to slide her clitoris up the shaft of her partner's penis on the backstroke, onto his pubic bone as she slides forward. At the same time, there is minimal stimulation for the man. He should not thrust, remaining totally relaxed as he lies passively on his back.

Once the man feels he can risk some movement, he can join in for short periods of time... then ease off, take a break, and settle down. As long as he is tracking his level of excitement, he can allow his partner to do her thing while he relaxes to regain control. Stopping the woman remains an option, should control threaten to be lost.

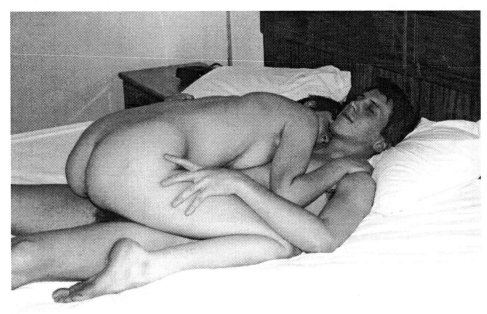

A nice variation of the female superior position is when the man reclines and the woman straddles him. This works best when the man's body is at an angle (not sitting and not flat) and the woman is doing the thrusting. Again, she has the opportunity to discover what is going to work best for her and, given the man's passivity and minimal stimulation, she has the time to explore. (A full page portrayal of this sitting/reclining position is presented later in this book.)

THE SCISSORS POSITION

I enthusiastically endorse the playful investigation of the benefits of the scissors position. In this position the woman lies flat on her back, with her partner on his side approaching almost at a right angle.

If he is right handed, he should be on his left side. He lifts the woman's right leg (the one closest to him) and, as he is making his penetration, he straddles her left leg with his two legs. Her right leg now comes down and rests across his right hip.

Most people look bewildered in hearing a verbal description of the scissors position, but upon seeing it the physical arrangement becomes clear. In fact, many couples have found the position on their own... just never had a name for it.

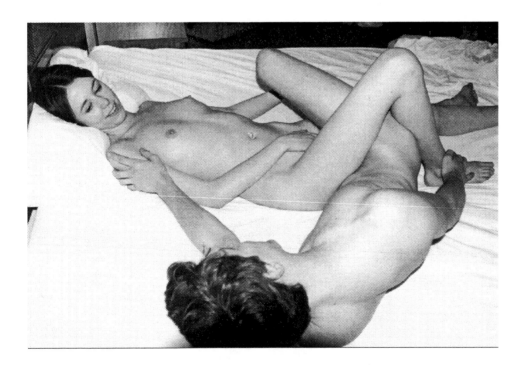

In this position, the man is relaxed and the urge for prolonged rapid thrusting is not triggered... in fact, the man's position is not even conducive to vigorous movement. The elements of control are here... relaxation and limited movement. It is a position in which the man can lie back and look at his partner's face and breasts, while manually stimulating her clitoris. He need only move enough to maintain his arousal while exciting his partner with his fingers, moving her along toward her orgasm. If he has learned to read her body and has learned to correctly interpret his own physical messages, he might just learn to time his orgasm to coincide with hers. Simultaneous orgasms are actually quite rare, but expertise in the scissors position might lead to a well-timed mutual explosion.

In the scissors position, the woman might actually be able to bring herself to orgasm by manually stimulating her own clitoris. This frees the man to more closely monitor his level of excitement and to reach over and, when safe, caress his partner's breast. Again, good timing might result in a simultaneous orgasm... but don't make that a requirement!

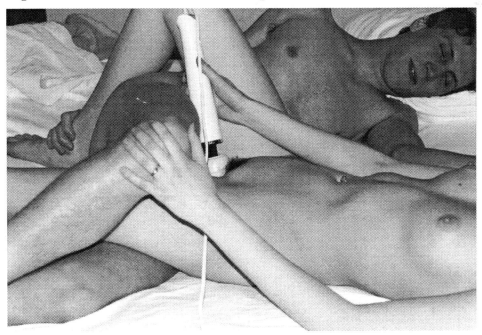

In the scissors position the woman can easily use her favorite vibrator on her clitoris, almost surely bring herself to orgasm while holding her partner's penis inside. He should make minimal movement, waiting to feel her hypertonicity begin to build. He can quicken his pace as she approaches her climax, thrusting vigorously as she breaks over the top and begins to orgasm.

THE SIDE BY SIDE POSITIONS

Any position that places the man on his side will be a position in which the man is more likely to be relaxed and one in which he can thrust lazily. You can always enjoy prolonged copulation in a pleasurable relaxed position and then switch to a "hotter" more vigorous one for the final scene.

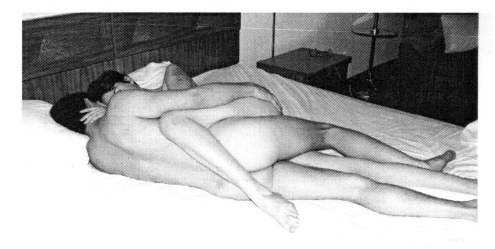

Take advantage of the lazy positions to talk. Thrust slowly, stop and relax. Tease with touch and words. It has been said that "The eyes are the window to the soul." Look deeply into each other's soul as you experience the combined warmth of your bodies. Feel the textures of your partner's skin, the caress of her vagina around your penis. Keep track of your arousal, but find words to tell her how good she feels... and how good she makes you feel.

Rush nothing now. Reminisce of past pleasures. Share your fantasies of future adventures. Celebrate the eroticism you both can share, but be careful. Monitor those inner signals. Better to rest and "soak" than to yield to that urge to thrust.

THE REAR ENTRY POSITIONS

A variation of the side by side position is the one in which the couple are lying front to back... in the *spoon position*. With the man in back, the closer his chest to his partner's back, the more shallow his penetration. For easier control, shallow penetration might be preferred. In holding his partner he can caress a breast

or may even be able to manually stimulated her clitoris. Relax to prolong this intimate coupling.

As the man moves his upper body away from his partner his penetration goes deeper. This position looks like a couple "doin' it doggie style" on their sides. It is a position that can lead easily into the scissors position, as the woman can roll over on her back, lifting her leg to lay over her partner's hip to make this transition.

The traditional rear entry position has the woman on her knees and the man behind, making entry from behind his partner. In this position the woman may be on her hands and knees.

I would offer one word of caution. Some women feel detached from there partner in this position... after all, she can not look up into his face. If your partner finds this "animalistic" or impersonal, find other positions that are mutually pleasurable. Be sure to ask, however, as there are also those women who love the position because it allows deep penetration and may indeed tap into a very old biological program. Be careful though... if it is an old program for the women, it's the same program Mother Nature gave to men!

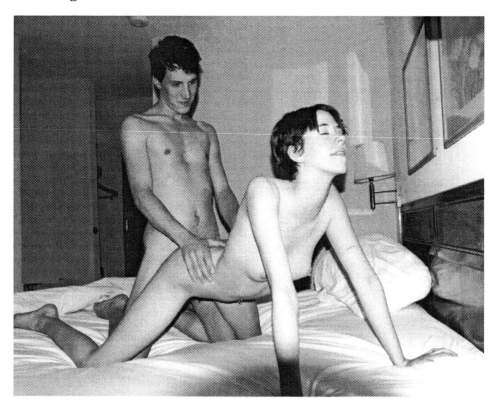

The woman may also let the top portion of her body drop down, resting her weight on her elbows. Be careful, as this tightens the vaginal grip around the penis. Thrust slowly and stay in touch with those inner physical signals.

Whether the woman is on her hands or on her elbows, it is absolutely essential that the man with a history of rapid ejaculation be extremely careful when kneeling behind his partner. There is an urge to grasp the woman's hips and thrust hard and deep... sure to trigger a quick ejaculation. To effectively use this position for prolonged intercourse you must stay in close, making slow short strokes.

Many women enjoy having a vibrator held on their clitoris while in the doggie position. Battery operated vibrators work fine, but some women prefer the more intense stimulation of an electric one. Remember, the advantage to using a vibrator or adding manual stimulation is that you can rest and maintain control while your partner progresses toward her climax. It would not take you long to catch up and join her in simultaneous orgasms.

As you gain a sense of confidence and control, you can quicken your stroke... just a few rapid long deep thrusts. A change of pace feels good to both partners, but you must maintain the monitoring of your excitement level. Alternate slow shallow thrusts with a few controlled deep rapid ones. Be very careful!

Be playful and creative in your exploration of other positions, remembering to stay in close and slowing your pace. Keep track, have fun and enjoy!

Periodic breaks can be taken when you lean forward to fondle a breast or to reach under your partner to caress her clitoris. This is the most risky of the positions recommended here, and requires that you keep close track of your level of excitement and to silence Mother Nature when she seductively whispers, "Grab hold and pound away."

While you might reach around to caress your partner's clitoris, she might find that it is more effective to stimulate herself. This relieves you of the responsibility of trying to maintaining control while, at the same time, pleasuring your partner. Furthermore, as a woman is the true expert on her own body, she often will take over to apply just that right touch to just the right spot.

Chapter 12

THE MESSAGES
TO BE LEARNED

FIRST THINGS FIRST - Fix the Relationship

It has happened more than once that a man will come into my office alone, complaining of premature ejaculation. Upon inquiry I will find that he has a life-long history of uncontrolled ejaculations, certainly evident through all of his current marriage (or long term relationship). At my request he brings his partner in for the next session. I will typically open with some statement like "Your husband (boyfriend) and I have talked about his concerns with rapid ejaculation." Then I'll ask, "How do you see this problem?"

I am no longer surprised when the woman responds, "I am going to leave him, not because he comes too fast, but because he is never home, he is verbally abusive, he drinks too much, he's a horrible father, and he has not worked in years! We've not had sex in 6 months and I will never have sex with him again!"

This is an unfortunate example of how some men seem to believe that the most important aspect in a relationship is good sex and if that can be fixed, everything else will fall into place. Of course most women feel that unless everything else is in place, there can be no good sex. After years of drifting apart and months of sleeping in separate bedrooms, there are men who had not perceived the depth of their partners' upset until they announced it in my office... and it becomes clear that what they needed was an attorney, not a sex therapist! The time to learn ejaculatory control is not in the midst of a rapidly deteriorating relationship. If the shoe fits, **fix the relationship before trying to fix the sex!**

Sexuality without sensuality, touch void of passion, and sex simply for the sake of an orgasm follow a primitive hardwired program, but are hollow human experiences. Emotional detachment, fear of intimacy, lack of knowledge, and inability to communicate will rob the sexual encounter of its richness. **Before beginning to work on mechanical sexual techniques, positions or endurance, perfect your ability to touch your partner in an intimate way... with your hands, with your words and with your heart.** A good screw will last only as long as the afterglow lasts, but good loving will last for a lifetime!

FIRST THINGS FIRST - Fix the Erection

As has been noted several times, performance anxiety can escalate to a near panic level and wipe out any chance of a stable erection. A man can usually identify this "stage fright," often claiming to get good erections when fully dressed and while making out on the living room couch. The fear of failure hits with the unbuttoning of a blouse in the bedroom... his penis suddenly rolls over and plays dead! He's suffering from the "*I gotta!*" syndrome. "*I gotta get it up!*"

It often happens that intercourse is rushed at the first sign that penetration might be possible... a decision based on his firmness, and not on her wetness. "*I gotta get it in!*" Although not aroused, the woman is often a co-conspirator in the hurried penetration, as she would rather deal with some vaginal discomfort than have to deal with his disappointment should he lose the shaky erection he has. "*I gotta keep it going!*"

With all their joint anxiety and with this rush into intercourse, one of two things is likely... the erection will fade even after penetration or he will ejaculate rapidly! Neither partner will be happy with either alternative, but will continue in each subsequent encounter to focus on getting him up and getting him in. If that is accomplished, they'll take their chances and just try even harder the next time!

If there is erectile unreliability because of sky high anxiety and a terrible fear of failure, something has to change. When there is both an erectile dysfunction and uncontrolled ejaculation, the focus can not be on improving endurance... pressure to perform was the culprit to begin with. **Fix the erection problem before trying to fix the rapid ejaculation!**

FILLING IN THOSE GAPS

As we have seen, while not the only factor nor necessarily the most important, waiting too long between ejaculations makes control a bit tougher. To illustrate the idea of increasing the frequency, I often tell the following story of two villagers and the frequency of their trips to the well...

Once upon a time there were two men who lived in the same small village. Each lived a half-mile from the well that supplied the only fresh water to the villagers. To get to this well the people of the village would run through a dark scary forest and, after filling their buckets, would then run home.

The first man made the trip to the well two or three times a week, filling his bucket to about the half-way mark. With his bucket less than full he could run swiftly home without spilling a drop. On arrival he could then dump the entire contents so that he and his wife could both enjoy the results of his treacherous journey.

The second man only made the trip to the well once a month. He and his wife would become quite thirsty as a result of his infrequent trips. Therefore, he would hurriedly fill his bucket to the brim and run home just as fast as he could. Unfortunately, on each of his return trips he could only run a short distance before all the water spilled from its container. His wife was disappointed by how little he could deliver!

The difference between the first man who always made it home successfully and the second man who always lost control along the way was not the size of the buckets, but the frequency of their trips to the well!

Birch (1996), *A Sex Therapist's Manual*

If your level of desire is stronger than that of your partner, masturbate between encounters and if you have time, practice the start/stop exercise. Do not embellish your masturbation in any way that would offend your partner. If, for example, she is uncomfortable with you watching adult videos, do not do so! Never risk damaging your relationship in the process of filling in the gaps. Hopefully, however, she will understand your greater need and accept that your masturbation is not a negative statement about her... rather that it is a beneficial tactic performed in the interest of the relationship.

It is always nice when a woman will allow her partner to lay beside her and masturbate, although I will admit that most couples would be somewhat uncomfortable with this. We have grown up with masturbation being such a taboo behavior and something always practiced in private. Going public with a partner can be tough... but as I said, it is nice if it can happen. If the women is comfortable holding the man, his brief masturbation becomes a shared activity in which she was not required to make a major investment. This would be one of those times when quick may be good!

Sometimes when there is a desire discrepancy between the partners, the one who seems to want sex less has an "ignition problem." The starter is broken, but the motor will run OK. While a mounting sexual desire is usually the starter, some folks (male and female) do not experience that spontaneous horny urge. Without a starter, they feel no need to be sexual. However, under the right circumstances and with the right touch, a jump start can get their motor running.

Remember the sensate focus homework? Remember the importance of a non-demand approach, with no pressure to respond and an emphasis on relaxation and pleasure. Quite often in scheduling sensual massage sessions a couple will discover the erotic joy of a slow caress and a gentle exchange of verbal feedback. If it is the woman who has the ignition problem, there should be no pressure and, after a full body massage, if the clitoris is touched in just the right way it might jump start her motor. A good artificial water soluble lubricant, such as **Astroglide**, works magic when lightly caressing an otherwise dry clitoris. The woman must give directions, get the kind of touching that feels best, and always have the right to say "It's not going to work, let's snuggle and you can masturbate yourself."

If there is a serious discrepancy in levels of desire, negotiating a mutually comfortable frequency and developing a "jump start" strategy is very crucial. **At times it is more important to work on getting one motor started than it is to focus on how long another will run!**

There is no pressure when it is OK to become aroused and OK not to become aroused; OK to orgasm and OK not to orgasm!! This is a "fail-safe" approach to sexuality... **sex is not about scoring, it's not a competitive sport and there is no place for the negative concept of failure in our bedrooms!!**

KEEP TRACK OF WHERE YOU'RE GOING

There are many things that will help manage your tendency to come quickly, but ultimately your ability to delay orgasm depends on your skill in keeping track of where you are on that climb toward the point of ejaculatory inevitability. You must be able to focus your attention inward and respond to the signals your body is giving you. Sense it... track it... control it! Do not risk ejaculating too soon by allowing yourself to get too close to that point of no return. You need not give up all pleasure, for you will find in time that you can slow down, close your eyes, change the pace, or move to a new position Stop when necessary... you must keep track and do something that will disrupt Mother Nature's old procreation program.

FOOLIN' OLD MOTHER NATURE

Let's review the hard-wired program... that get it up, get it in, get it off sequence. It begins with desire and there is that natural visual attraction to our mate and possibly other persons of the same gender. There is the flight into La La Land followed closely with an urgent drive to mount and penetrate. Then those built-in pelvic thrusts kick in once we have surrounded our penis with the warmth of our partner. While in motion our bodies tense briefly as we race toward the point of ejaculatory inevitability. As programed, our seminal vesicles and prostate contract, we feel an internal squish and, in less than a second we come!

So, that's Ma Nature's program and here's your final plan. Schedule your encounters so that you have plenty of opportunity to play and so that your physical intimacy does not become lost in a hurried encounter. Start out with enough time to relax and caress sensually before moving on to the sexual touch. Take turns touching... giving and receiving. Keep track and stay relaxed. **Give feedback about what feels good, but never forget to stop the stimulation before reaching that point of ejaculatory inevitability.**

Schedule your encounters at a comfortable frequency and, if needed fill the gaps with masturbation. Remember, the longer the duration between orgasms, the more difficult it will be to maintain control.

If at any time you feel that tingly about-to-explode feeling, announce it and walk it off if necessary... if it feels like the first touch will make you come, it probably will, so don't risk it. Get up and get settled!!

If your partner is more likely to orgasm with oral or manual stimulation, give her the opportunity to choose... she can have her orgasm(s) before intercourse or she can wait to see how things go. Remember, you can always come back to help her orgasm after intercourse or, if she is comfortable, she can finish the job herself while you are holding her.

During the foreplay, continue to "informally" do the start/stop and communicate erotic desires to each others... and those gentle helpful directions, such as "slowly now my love," "be careful with that spot," "go easy now," etc. But always remember, yelling "stop" is better than having to muttering "Oh shit!"

Be sure you are under control before making penetration. Remember my recommendation that intercourse be in the female superior position. You partner should slowly lower herself down on to you and just sit quietly! Mother Nature wants you to begin thrusting, so DO NOT MOVE! Once you sense you are under control, signal your partner to begin, but you remain perfectly still. Do not allow your body to tighten or tense in any way. **Remember, in the early coital encounters, don't dare thrust... stay as relaxed as humanly possible.**

Let her move on you while you are just keeping track!! Getting excited... close you eyes...Mother Nature made her body attractive to you, so do not watch her! Feeling great... Mother Nature is giving you a one-way ticket to La La Land, so think of those unpaid taxes! Getting close... the natural program dictates

"Go for those long fast strokes," so keep your partner in close and slow her down. Remember, when you feel you are getting close to that point of no return, stop... right now! Breath deeply and relax... feel yourself coming down that imaginary ladder.

Once back under control, tell your partner to start again, but continue to keep track, starting and stopping, until you want to come. Continue to schedule your time together, but remember, you can still have spontaneous sessions between your planned encounters and you can still have "quickies" when that is what you both want.

Begin playing with other positions and vary your stroking once it becomes safe for you to become more active. Experiment with what you are able to manage without losing control... learn to hover at a nice level of arousal... but always keep track. **Remember, although there is no cure, you can learn to manage your response, and a lesson well learned will be good forever!**

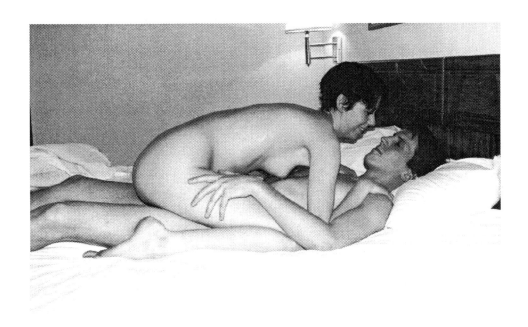

Chapter 13

CONCLUSIONS

In 1977 a publication appeared on bookshelves entitled *The Last Sex Manual*. From the title, one would have thought that this book was so comprehensive, so insightful, and so well written that no one could ever again write another book about sex. I am sure that hundreds of sex manuals have been written in the 20 years since that publication. Some of what appears in print is simply a rehashing of what had been written before... simply "old wine in new skins." However, I am also convinced that each author has presented the material in their own unique way, and that from time to time there have been not only new words, but some new concepts.

Our sexuality is such a personal possession, an integral (although private) part of who we are. When sexuality is not talked of in an open and honest manner, we may at times wonder if we really know all that we might know, or we might be uncertain that what we are experiencing is all that we are really capable of experiencing. We may wonder if others think the same as we think, feel just as we feel, and revel in what we have found to be pleasurable. It is out of this curiosity that many people who had purchased and studied that very last sex manual went out and bought another... and another.

Within the sea of books on sexuality, there are relatively few manuscripts devoted specifically to a self-help program for rapid ejaculators. However, for the most part, those that have been written are very good. The writing style of other authors will differ from mine, the understanding of the process of arousal will vary, and the homework will emphasize aspects or techniques I have minimized or abandoned. While I may even disagree with some writers, you should read all that you can read, as different perspectives can only broaden your appreciation of this aspect of your being... an aspect that has troubled you so. Playfully share the books with your partner and together, develop a plan that you agree might work for you. It can be fun!

It is important to feel OK about yourself... to end any guilt or shame, to give up any feelings of inadequacy or failure. Rapid ejaculation is not an illness and management of your arousal is quite possible. Negative feelings are of no value and only channel your attention into self criticism, not constructive change. Dr. Marian Dunn, in the video entitled *You Can Last Longer*, says that "Being a good lover depends on a man's desire to please, good communication, practice, patience and imagination... not just his ejaculatory control." Remember, if you are in a relationship, it is essential that you work creatively and cooperatively to enhance both your physical and emotional intimacy, and not focus just on learning control. The good news is that you can work on all of this at the same time!

Make time to be playful and, in your sensual exchange, learn all you can about each other. Be curious as you openly share erotic desires and help each other discover what really feels good. Celebrate the passion, perfect your art of giving, and make a commitment to always nurture physical and emotional intimacy. Your sexuality can become a joyful life-long pleasure if you accept a **fail safe philosophy**, moving away from the *goal of just making intercourse* and discovering the joy of the intimate *process of making love.*

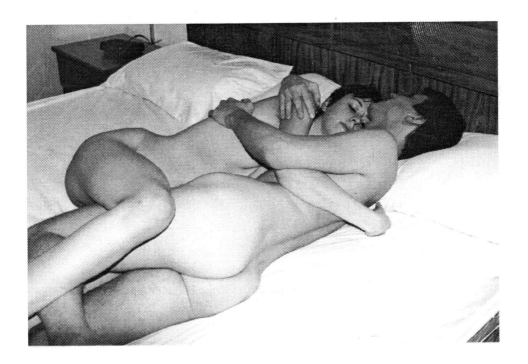

RAPID EJACULATION SELF ASSESSMENT

Your response to the following questions may assist you in clarifying or better understanding your concerns about premature or rapid ejaculation. Respond to each question as truthfully and completely as you can, answering as you really feel or think, not as you believe you should.

1. Is your problem with rapid ejaculation a new one? **(YES) (NO)** If **YES**, when did it seem to start?

    _____

    _____

2. Is your problem a chronic one [life long] **(YES) (NO)** If **YES**, what have you tried in the past to gain better control?_____

    _____

3. How often are you attempting to have intercourse? _____ Who typically initiates?

    _____

3. How long does the foreplay typically last before any penetration is made?_____ Is there anything about the type or duration of foreplay that seems to influence your control?

    _____

4. Do you ever ejaculate just **prior** to penetration? (**YES**) (**NO**) If **YES**, what percent of the time?_____%

5. Do you ever ejaculate **immediately** upon penetration? (**YES**) (**NO**) If **YES**, what percent of the time?_____%

6. If you can accomplish penetration, how quickly are you ejaculating once you begin intercourse? _____(minutes) (seconds)

7. What percent of the time do **you** feel you have ejaculated too quickly?_____% What percent of the time does your **partner** think you were too quick?_____%

8. Do you ever get a second erection and ejaculate a second time? (**YES**) (**NO**) If **YES**, how often does this occur?_____ If you experience a second ejaculation, how long can you last once intercourse begins?_____

9. Do you masturbate? (**YES**) (**NO**) If **YES**, how often?_____ How long are you lasting with this **self** stimulation?_____ _____ If you control your ejaculation during masturbation, how are you doing this?_____

    _____

10. Is you partner comfortable stimulating you manually during foreplay? (**YES**) (**NO**) If **YES**, how long do you last with your **partner's** manual stimulation?

    _____

11. Is your partner comfortable with giving oral stimulation? (**YES**) (**NO**) If YES, how long do you last when orally stimulated?

    _____

12. During foreplay, do you worry about ejaculating with this preliminary touching? (**YES**) (**NO**) Do you worry about ejaculating too rapidly before even beginning foreplay? (**YES**) (**NO**) Is there anything about your level of anxiety or stress that seems to influence your control ?_____

    _____

13. How often do you desire sex?_____
    How often does your partner desire_____
    Do you ever avoid initiating sex because of a fear of
    ejaculating too rapidly? (**YES**) (**NO**) If **YES**, how
    frequent is this?_____

15 Are you experiencing any problems obtaining or
    maintaining an erection? (**YES**) (**NO**) If **YES**, do you
    ever ejaculate rapidly even though your penis is not
    hard? (**YES**) (**NO**) Do you ever ejaculate before you
    feel fully aroused? (**YES**) (**NO**)

16. Does the position of intercourse make a difference,
    i.e., can you last longer in some positions than in
    others? (**YES**) (**NO**) If **YES**, what positions?

    _____

    What do you think the difference is?

    _____
    _____

17. Do you have more than one partner? (**YES**) (**NO**) If
    YES, can you last longer with one than with another?
    (**YES**) (**NO**) If **YES**, what do you think the difference
    is?_____

    _____

18. What is your reaction when you ejaculate rapidly?_____

_____

What is your partner(s) reaction when it happens?

_____

19. Are you bringing your partner to orgasm before you ejaculate, or after?_____ If neither, why not?_____ Does everything stop once you have ejaculated? (**YES**) (**NO**) If **YES**, who wants to stop - you, your partner or both?

_____

20. What have you attempted in the past to gain better control or to last longer? _____

_____

_____ Has anything seemed to help?

_____

21. Has any partner compared you with another lover, e.g., "He could last an hour, why can't you?" (**YES**) (**NO**) Has any partner questioned your love, e.g., "If you loved me you would last longer to satisfy me." (**YES**) (**NO**) If **YES**, how have you reacted?

_____

_____

22. Has any partner attempted to reassure you, e.g., "It doesn't matter," or "I loved all the rest of it." (**YES**) (**NO**) If **YES**, how have you reacted?

_____

23. Do you believe this is a physical problem, a psychological problem, or a combination of both?_____

24. Have you sought help for this concern in the past? (**YES**)(**NO**) What was recommended and what did you try? _____

_____

Add any additional thoughts here

PROFESSIONAL RESOURCES

If you find that you are unable to gain satisfactory control on your own or if your relationship is in serious trouble because of your rapid ejaculation or other sexual concerns, do not hesitate to consult a **qualified** sexuality therapist or counselor. If there are no other relationship issues, a well trained and experienced sex therapist can assist you in a relatively brief period of time. To locate a qualified professional in your geographic area, write to one or both of the following national certificating associations:

American Academy of Clinical Sexology
1929 18th Street NW, Suite 1166
Washington, DC 20009

American Association of Sex Educators, Counselors
   and Therapists
P.O. Box 238
Mt. Vernon, IA 52314

REFERENCES

Abrams, P., (1979). How to Cure Premature Ejaculation, April Issue, *Forum*.

Birch, R., (1996). *Oral Caress: The Loving Guide to Exciting a Woman*. Columbus: PEC Publishing.

Birch, R., (1996). *A Sex Therapist's Manual*. Columbus: PEC Publishing.

Bixler, R., (1986). Of Apes and Men (Including Females!). *Journal of. Sex Research*, vol 22, 255-267.

Eichel, E. & Nobile, P., (1992). *The Perfect Fit*. New York: Fine.

Gebhard, P., (1996). Factors in Marital Orgasm. *Journal of Social Issues*, vol 22, 88-95.

Grenier, G. & Byers, S., (1995). Rapid Ejaculation: A Review of Conceptual, Etiological, and Treatment Issues, *Archives of Sexual Behavior*, Vol. 24, No. 4., 447-472.

Hong, L., (1984). Survival of the Fastest: On the Origin of Premature Ejaculation. *Journal of Sex Research*, vol 20, 109-112.

Junot, D., (1995). Stop Premature Ejaculation and Learn to Control Male Orgasm, Metairie, LA: Sex-Press.

Kaplan, H. S., (1974). *The New Sex Therapy.* New York: Brunner/Mazel.

Kaplan, H. S., (1989). *PE: How to Overcome Premature Ejaculation.* New York: Brunner/Mazel.

Kinsey, A., Pomeroy, W., & Martin, C., (1948). *Sexual Behavior in the Human Male.* Philadelphia: W. B. Saunders.

Laumann, E., Gagnon, J., Michael, R. & Michaels, S., (1994) *The Social Organization of Sexuality: Sexual Practices in the United States.* Chicago: University of Chicago Press.

Levins, H.., (1989) *American Sex Machines,* Holbrook, MA: Adams Media.

Masters, W. & Johnson, V., (1966). *Human Sexual Response.* Boston: Little, Brown & Company.

Masters W. & Johnson, V., (1970). *Human Sexual Inadequacy.* Boston: Little Brown & Company.

Pion, R., (1977). *The Last Sex Manual.* New York: Wyden Books.

Rouleau, J. (1990). Sexotherapy and Disorders of Ejaculation. *Acta Urol Belg*, vol. 57, 191-194.

Safir, M. (1997) Personal correspondence.

Vickery, D. & Fries, J., (1996). Take Care of Yourself. Addison-Wesley.

Zilbergeld, B., (1992). *The New Male Sexuality.* New York: Bantam Books.

You Can Last Longer: Solutions for Ejaculatory Control. (1992). *Better Sex Video Series,*Vol. 8, Sinclair Institute, P.O. Box 8865, Chapel Hill, NC 27515.

REFERENCES

ABOUT THE AUTHOR

Dr. Robert Birch received his Ph.D. from the University of Wisconsin in 1967 and has been a practicing psychologist for 30 years. Following 10 years of clinical experience in public mental health agencies he entered into independent practice and began what is now a 20 year specialty in marital and sex therapy. He has characterized his professional interests as centering around intimate and caring emotional and physical relationships.

Dr. Birch is a Fellow of the American Academy of Family Psychology, a Fellow and Approved Supervisor of the American Association for Marriage and Family Therapy [AAMFT], and a Clinical Fellow and Supervisor of the American Academy of Clinical Sexologists. He is a Diplomate of the American Board of Sexology and has been certified as a Sex Therapist, Sex Educator and Supervisor by the American Association of Sex Educators, Counselors and Therapists [AASECT]. He is also certified as a Family Therapist by the National Academy of Certified Family Therapists [NACFT]. He holds membership in the American Psychological Association [APA], the Ohio Psychological Association [OPA], the Society for the Scientific Study of Sexuality [SSSS], the Society for Sex Therapy and Research [SSTAR], and the Sexuality Information and Education Council of the United States [SIECUS]. He has served on the Examining Board of the American Board of Family Psychology and on the national and state Board of Directors of both AAMFT and AASECT.

Dr. Birch has held multiple consulting positions with church counseling groups, public social service agencies, and with the United States Air Force. In 1988 he was honored as a "Distinguished Visiting Professor" by the Wilford Hall Medical Center at the Lackland Air Force Base in San Antonio, Texas. He has provided clinical supervision and has taught courses within the Family Therapy Program of The Ohio State University, where he holds the designation as an Adjunct Assistant Professor. He is the Supervising Psychologist for the Beechwold Family Counseling Associates in Columbus, Ohio, and is the Director of Professional Education Consultants and PEC Publishing.

Dr. Birch has presented over 400 public lectures and professional seminars and has authored scores of articles. He has been interview multiple times on television, has been a regular guest on a late night call-in radio program, and has been quoted extensively in newspapers, books and magazines. He has written five client education pamphlets as "consumer guides." He is the author of a 1996 adult sex education book entitled *Oral Caress: The Loving Guide to Exciting a Woman* and a clinical workbook for professionals entitled *A Sex Therapist's Manual*. Information about all PEC publications may be found on the Internet at the web site address **http://www.oralcaress.com**.

Dr. Birch has dedicated his clinical skills, his public speaking, and his writing to the enhancement of healthy sensuality and sexuality, believing in the importance of a solid physical and emotional bond in the maintenance of long term relationships.

Index